Finns

IN MINNESOTA

Arnold R. Alanen

Minnesota Historical
Society Press

Dedicated to the memory of my parents and immigrant maternal grandparents who exposed me to Finnish language and culture on a farm in northeastern Minnesota. They lived their lives believing in the cooperative movement as a path to the common good.

www.mhspress.org

The Minnesota Historical Society Press is a member of the Association of American University Presses.

Manufactured in the United States of America

10 9 8 7 6 5 4 3 2

♾ The paper used in this publication meets the minimum requirements of the American National Standard for Information Sciences—Permanence for Printed Library Materials, ANSI Z39.48-1984.

International Standard Book Number
ISBN: 978-0-87351-854-3 (paper)
ISBN: 978-0-87351-860-4 (e-book)

Library of Congress Cataloging-in-Publication Data

Alanen, Arnold R. (Arnold Robert)
    Finns in Minnesota / Arnold R. Alanen.
        p. cm. — (The people of Minnesota)
    Includes bibliographical references and index.
        ISBN 978-0-87351-854-3 (pbk. : alk. paper) — ISBN 978-0-87351-860-4 (e-book)
        1. Finns—Minnesota—History. 2. Finns—Minnesota—Social conditions. 3. Finland-Swedes—Minnesota—History. 4. Finland-Swedes—Minnesota—Social conditions. 5. Finnish Americans—Minnesota—History. 6. Finnish Americans—Minnesota—Social conditions. 7. Minnesota—Ethnic relations—History. 8. Finland—Emigration and immigration—History. 9. Minnesota—Emigration and immigration—History. I. Title.
F615.F5A53   2012
305.89'45410776—dc23

                                                                                2011053467

Front cover: Finnish lumber camp, northeastern Minnesota. Institute of Migration, Turku, Finland
Back cover: First cousins Ailie Kurkinen and Carl Orjala at the John and Maria Orjala farm, East Lake, Minnesota, 1934. Photo courtesy of the Carl Orjala family.

Cover design by Running Rhino Design.
Book design and composition by Wendy Holdman.

Contents

A group of young Finnish Minnesotans frolic in the snow at the John and Mary Rengo farm in Automba Township (Carlton County), c. 1910.

Finns

IN MINNESOTA

More than three hundred thousand Finns settled in the United States from 1864 to 1914, but thousands of others returned to Finland, including Alajärvi blacksmith Aaron Tallbacka, who left his wife and two children at home when sailing for Duluth, the "Helsinki of America," in 1910. A few years later, Tallbacka returned to Alajärvi and opened a blacksmith forge that he called *Tuluuti* (Duluth); the site was later accessed along *Tuluutintie* (Duluth Road), still identified by this road sign in 2011.

IN THE EARLY SUMMER OF 1864, a group of Finnish immigrants, numbering at least seventeen, stepped off a Mississippi River steamboat and onto Minnesota soil at Red Wing. They weren't the first Finns to arrive in North America, a place they called *Suuri Länsi,* or the "Great West"; since the 1600s, small numbers of Finns had immigrated to North America and scattered across the continent. But the 1864 immigrants, along with other Finns who came later that summer, were the first to arrive as groups with the intent to settle permanently in a specific place—Minnesota. (A small number of Finnish miners may have made their way to northern Michigan in 1864, but definitive proof of their arrival does not appear until 1865.) As a consequence, these Minnesota Finns served as the vanguard for more than three hundred thousand Finnish émigrés who settled in the United States from 1864 to 1914.

Red Wing was but a brief way station for the Finns before they moved on to settle in south-central Minnesota. They were followed by about five hundred other Finns who arrived from the mid-1860s to the 1880s and who also settled in the south-central counties of Renville, Wright, and Meeker, as well as in Minneapolis and the west-central counties of Douglas, Otter Tail, Wadena, and Becker. The flow of Finnish immigrants expanded noticeably from the late 1880s to 1914. At this time, however, most streamed into northeastern Minnesota, where they settled in urban Duluth and the logging camps, mines, mills, and rural settlements of St. Louis, Carlton, Itasca, Lake, and Aitkin counties; smaller contingents moved to Crow Wing, Pine, and Koochiching counties. By 1920 these eight northeastern counties included 80 percent of the 29,110 Finns who resided in Minnesota; 60 percent were in St. Louis County alone.

Immigrant Numbers

Sweden ruled Finland until 1809, when it became an autonomous Grand Duchy of the Russian Empire; Finland achieved independence in late 1917, once Russian rule ended. Because of Finland's status as a Grand Duchy, U.S. officials grouped Finns with Russians when preparing nineteenth-century census reports. Indeed, the original 1870 and 1880 manuscript census schedules (those for 1890 no longer exist) used to compile the reports reveal that some enumerators wrote down "Russia" when noting a Finn's place of birth, and numerous Finns were not counted at all. Finnish American groups called for changes during the 1890s, arguing that Finland was not a province of Russia, that Finland was "independent in domestic matters," and that "Finns and Russians were entirely different races." Federal officials concurred, and Finns were listed as a separate nationality group in published census reports from 1900 onward. Nonetheless, the directive was not always followed, as revealed by one 1910 census enumerator who listed 295 Finns in the St. Louis County townships of Alango, Angora, and Sturgeon as Russians. In addition, a significant proportion of early Finnish émigrés were born in either northern Sweden or Norway and are included with the published counts for those two countries. As a result, Finns are underrepresented in nineteenth- and early-twentieth-century censuses.[1]

Minnesota has had the nation's second-largest Finnish population since the early 1880s, trailing only Michigan. A total of 10,725 Finns lived in Minnesota by 1900—8,185 fewer than in Michigan. When Minnesota's Finnish numbers reached 26,635 in 1910, the differential declined to 4,510, and it then narrowed to 985 in 1920 when the Minnesota total peaked at 29,110. Throughout this period and up to the present day, however, Minnesota has claimed the nation's highest proportion of Finnish residents in its population. Finns constituted two to three percent of the

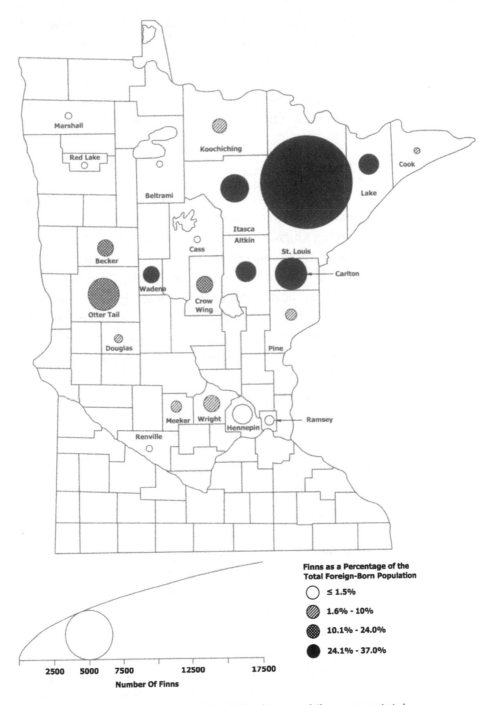

Marshall

Red Lake

Koochiching

Cook

Beltrami

Lake

Becker

Itasca
Aitkin

Cass

St. Louis

Wadena

Carlton

Crow
Wing

Otter Tail

Douglas

Pine

Meeker Wright

Ramsey

Hennepin

Renville

**Finns as a Percentage of the
Total Foreign-Born Population**

○ ≤ 1.5%

◍ 1.6% - 10%

⬤ 10.1% - 24.0%

● 24.1% - 37.0%

2500   5000   7500   12500   17500

Number Of Finns

By 1920, almost 80 percent of Minnesota's Finnish immigrant population was concentrated
in eight northeastern counties.

state's foreign-born populace during the first decades of the twentieth century. Two percent (99,400) of all Minnesotans claimed some Finnish ancestry by 2000, while Michigan's 101,350 people of Finnish descent represented one percent of its population. A recent survey estimates that the 2010 figure for Minnesota's Finns stood at 97,850.

A Finnish Presence in Minnesota

Despite their relatively small overall numbers, Finns have been concentrated within a few sections of Minnesota, earning a higher profile in these areas. People residing outside of these concentrations may still have some knowledge of Minnesota's "Finnishness"—very likely the *sauna,* the Finns' most visible cultural marker. Some may know of *sisu,* which refers to the Finns' tenacity when dealing with extremely difficult circumstances. Others may recognize the road signs that display Finnish names in Minnesota's northern half, or the ninety or so terms that officially identify places and geographic sites. Another form of identity occurs on St. Urho's Day, a March event that celebrates a mythical saint who was invented in Minnesota during the 1950s and which is now celebrated in many North American Finnish communities. Sports fans have watched numerous Finns play for Minnesota's professional hockey teams, and, since 2003, Finnish native Osmo Vänskä, director of the Minnesota Orchestra, has provided the state's citizens with an awareness of his country's vibrant musical culture.

Finns have made meaningful contributions to Minnesota's cultural, labor, political, religious, commercial, and intellectual life, but relatively limited physical evidence of these achievements is visible on the contemporary landscape. While few other groups were stronger proponents of cooperation as a way to achieve the "common good" (*yhteishyvä*), only a limited number of the Finns' original cooperative ventures—stores and gas stations, for example—exist today.

A waterfront site, such as this Duluth example, is considered the ideal location for a sauna. Designed by Duluth architect David Salmela, the sauna is both whimsical and poetic and displays a steeply pitched roof suggestive of Finnish farmhouses. The sauna received several state and national design awards following its completion in 2004.

Minnesota's Finns also sponsored more than 150 congregations and churches, most of them Lutheran; because of doctrinal differences, the congregations typically affiliated with one of three major Lutheran associations organized by America's Finns. Only one—the Laestadians or Apostolic Lutherans—still maintains a strong connection to its ethnic origins; the other two associations have been absorbed into large Lutheran synods. Nothing, however, more clearly speaks to the diverse views of Minnesota's Finnish community than politics.

Menahga's fiberglass St. Urho, portrayed here in 2010, is one of two statues that commemorate the fictitious Finnish saint in Minnesota; the other St. Urho statue, a wooden chain-sawed version, is located in northeastern Minnesota at Finland.

In fact, few ethnic groups of similar size have displayed such diversity—and turmoil—within their ranks. What other small Minnesota group has produced a Republican congressman and governor, the nation's first Communist mayor, and a four-time Communist Party of America candidate for U.S. president? Perhaps Finns do represent "America's largest dysfunctional family."[2]

This book begins with a brief summary of Finnish migration to North America before 1864 and follows with a discussion of factors that led several hundred thousand Finns to leave over the next half century. Most of the volume features the 1864–1945 period in Minnesota, although an overview of the post–World War II years is also provided. Since Minnesota has included numerous Finland Swedes—people born in Finland who speak Swedish—the book concludes with a portrait of this unique group. Because Finnish migration began in the far northern reaches of the Nordic world, a Finnish Sámi (Lapp) presence has also been evident in Minnesota. While it is estimated that thirty thousand Sámi immigrated to America, most from Norway and Sweden, an accurate count cannot be determined since they often hid their identity to avoid discrimination. Therefore, the number of Finnish Sámi who settled in Minnesota is unknown.[3]

Early Emigration from Finland

Significant emigration from Finland occurred during the 1500s and 1600s when more than ten thousand Finns, most from the eastern region of Savo-Karelia, departed for the uninhabited uplands of Värmland and west-central Sweden. Several hundred of these "Värmland Finns" assisted in establishing Sweden's Delaware River valley colonies throughout areas of present-day Delaware, Pennsylvania, New Jersey, and Maryland from the 1640s to the 1660s.[4]

Two centuries later, during the Russian era of Finnish

history, Alaska emerged as a destination for some ambitious and adventurous Finns, including two naval officers who served as the czars' governors. America's miniscule mid-nineteenth-century Finnish population was augmented by adventurers who departed after hearing of the 1849 California gold rush and sailors who left their ships at Pacific and Atlantic ports during the 1850s.[5]

Among the small but steady flow of Finns who began arriving in the United States from 1864 to the 1880s were at least five hundred whose birthplace was northern Norway; more than fifty settled in Minnesota, and at least another hundred left via Norwegian ports. Other early Finnish-speaking immigrants departed from the Swedish side of the Tornio River that separates Finland and Sweden. (No political boundary divided northern Finland and Sweden, but the Tornio became the official border following the Russian annexation of Finland.) Wherever their origins, Finnish-speaking émigrés typically expressed fidelity to Finland. Decades after reaching Minnesota during the mid-1860s, an elderly Finnish woman from northern Sweden compared her compatriots' sentiments to those immigrants who had arrived directly from their homeland: "Finland is as dear to us as you others," she emphasized.[6]

The Why and Where of Immigration

"America fever" (*Amerikankuume*), which gripped much of Finland by the early 1870s, was generally spurred by the same factors that led to the departure of tens of millions of Europeans between the 1820s and 1914. Although many people claim that Finns settled in Minnesota "because it looked like Finland," the major reason was economic. These "rural proletarians left to escape moneyless circumstances," and Minnesota's forests, farms, mines, towns, and cities offered employment opportunities during the Finns' major period of migration. Also of importance was a nineteenth-century population explosion caused by improvements in Finland's medical and health situation. When the number of Finns expanded from fewer than one million in 1800 to three million in 1914, the area of cultivated land failed to provide an adequate food supply for the "surplus population." The growth rate of the crofter or tenant farmer class exceeded that of landowners by two times, while the landless peasant group grew fivefold. As conditions became increasingly precarious, many peasants and crofters sought work by moving from farm to farm in Finland.[7]

During the mid-1890s, political oppression was added to the list of factors contributing to Finnish emigration. The 1835 publication of Finland's folk epic the *Kalevala* had already inspired a nationalistic awareness that led to Russian recognition of the Finnish language in 1863. When the Finns' political and cultural awakening grew throughout the 1890s, however, Czar Nicholas II eliminated Finland's autonomous status and threatened young males with conscription in the Russian military. Immigrant numbers quickly rose, increasing from 3,385 in 1898 to 12,995 in 1899 and then to a record 23,310 in 1902. Altogether, some 264,000 Finns, or 88 percent of all immigrants, departed between 1893 and 1914. About 39 percent belonged either to the tenant farmer or landless peasant classes, 30 percent

Finland's Famine Years of the 1860s

Despite Finland's nineteenth-century population gains, death rates spiked sharply upward during the famine years of 1866–68, when 15 percent of the population died. Three parishes—Ikaalinen, Kankaanpää, and Parkano—illustrate the severity of this period. The frigid spring of 1866 was followed by a summer with fifty continuous days of rain and the early arrival of winter; the next spring was so cold that snow remained on the ground by late May and iced-over lakes could support horses. When the crop yield of 1867 proved insufficient, people ate bread made from tree bark flour (*pettuleipä*). The three parishes experienced 4,750 deaths in 1867-68— 3,800 more than the previous seven years. With Finland often characterized as a place of "cold and bark bread," no wonder some Finns began thinking about America's possibilities.[i]

were farm owners and their families, 20 percent were "workers" (hired hands, maids, factory laborers), and 11 percent represented miscellaneous categories. More than one-half would come from *Pohjanmaa* (Ostrobothnia)—a west-central region of Finland that includes most of the Province of Vaasa and much of the Province of Oulu.[8]

While America may have been described as "hell for men and horses, but heaven for women," males clearly dominated the Finnish immigrant spectrum: 35 percent of Finland's émigrés were females, compared to Denmark's 39 percent, Norway's 41 percent, and Sweden's 45 percent. When contrasted with most eastern and southern European groups, however, the Finnish male-female ratio was more balanced.[9]

Since so many Finns departed during the late nineteenth and early twentieth centuries, historians do not include them with the "old immigrants" of Western Europe who comprised the majority of America's pre-1890s arrivals. Instead, Finns are typically grouped with the "new immigrants" of Eastern and Southern Europe: Italians, Jews, Poles, South Slavs, and so forth. Nevertheless, Finnish historian Reino Kero contends that Finland's migration situation is somewhat of an anomaly because it "does not seem to belong to the old any more than to the new immigration." Migration from Finland, therefore, represents a continuum of the old and new eras, although the majority of émigrés departed during the later period.[10]

While improving one's economic situation was primarily responsible for the Finns' decision to migrate, other factors existed, too, including family disputes, the disintegration of marriages, escaping commitments and arrangements, and animosity toward the state church. Some migrants simply sought adventure. "Finns have been just as curious as Columbus ... ever hoping for favorable places to live," wrote a Finnish American newspaperman in 1878. One year later, another Finn sardonically commented on the reasons for his temporary move to the United States: "I wanted to see the world and what other people do so that in my older days I could talk about more things than the elderly men in Savo who look at the sunrise from dung piles and listen to the cuckoo bird sing." [11]

Thousands of immigrant letters sent to Finland generated further interest in Minnesota and America. One 1868 letter published in a Finnish newspaper described Minnesota's positive qualities and included the writer's promise to assist any "dear brother" who immigrated:

> My major purpose this time is to offer you brotherly and honest information about this country's conditions and life. And now, my dear brother! Now I wish to invite you to come and reside here, to live, and to die. Leave your country of birth and come here my dear brother! If you are very rich, then it will be easier and better to get started. Therefore, I promise that I will be of assistance in preparing the soil so you might be my neighbor. No matter how good your life is there, here it is even better. [12]

Large contingents of Minnesota's Finns engaged in mining and timberwork, but an undeniable land hunger led a majority to farming. *Oma tupa, oma lupa* ("One's home, one's way") typified a dream embraced by many. Indeed, by 1920 Minnesota included 4,700 Finnish farms—the highest number in the nation and 755 more than in Michigan. [13]

Minnesota's First Rural Finnish Settlements: Franklin, Cokato, and Holmes City

The first seventeen Finns who arrived in 1864 included three families with eight young children among them: Peter and Johanna Lahti, Matti and Maria Niemi (Johnson), and Antti and Maria Rovainen. The youngest traveler was the Niemis'

Learning English, Speaking "Finglish"

Virtually all Finnish immigrants possessed a basic ability to read and write, making them among America's most literate ethnic groups. But since Finnish differs so significantly from Indo-European languages, Finns commonly found it difficult to master English; they did, however, develop their own North American language—*Finglish* or *Fingliska*—which employed English words within a Finnish grammatical framework (e.g., *kaara* for car, *petiruuma* for bedroom).

Church and Socialist organizations provided Finnish-language classes for the immigrants' children, although Virginia Finns who submitted a petition to their local school board in 1912 had a more ambitious goal: substituting Finnish for German as a foreign-language requirement since students with Finnish backgrounds exceeded the German group "by fully six times." The board later reported that German would continue because of college admission requirements, but if Finnish ever become mandatory, they would "gladly introduce" such a course.

Until the 1940s, children with Finnish backgrounds attending rural schools often spoke their ancestral language at home. This, complained a Swedish American mother from Brimson, contributed to a "prevailing brogue" and "the mutilation of the English language as it is spoken by children of foreign-speaking parents." Furthermore, she asserted, one could hear "Swedish children speak English with a Finnish accent." Bobby Aro, a popular songwriter, singer, and disc jockey from Zim who specialized in Finglish music, offered this observation in his whimsical 1957 recording "King of the Great Northwoods." Explaining his accent, Aro exclaims, "I'm not Finnish, but my English teacher was!"[ii]

These children of Finnish immigrants display their prizewinning potatoes outside the Idington school in rural St. Louis County, 1917.

baby son, born weeks before the family departed Norway. The others were three single men—Mikko Heikka, Matti Niemi, Jr., and Matti Nulus. Five adults were born in northern Finland, three in northern Sweden, and the eight children in Vadsø, Norway.[14]

After leaving Vadsø, the Finns embarked on an arduous three-month-long voyage, including transfers to different sailing vessels in Tromsø and Trondheim, Norway, and Liverpool, England. Following their transatlantic crossing, the group docked in Quebec, Canada, where they boarded a Great Lakes steamer for Chicago, followed by a train trip to La Crosse, Wisconsin, and then a short riverboat journey up the Mississippi to Red Wing. Seeking to avoid a severe cholera outbreak, the intrepid Finns moved southwestward to St. Peter.[15]

Two smaller groups landed later that year, and somewhat greater numbers arrived in 1865 and 1866. Several men found work nearby as woodcutters, but at least twenty-five Finns, including Briita Sukki and her five children, succumbed to cholera. Spurred by this scourge, most survivors also departed for St. Peter. There, a Norwegian Lutheran pastor encouraged them to move up the Minnesota River, where land for homesteading was available in the Renville County townships of Bandon, Camp, and Birch Cooley. Here they formed Minnesota's first Finnish *pesäpaikka* ("nesting place"). Peter Lahti was among the first farmers, but not until after he initially joined a Minnesota Union Army unit, along with the younger Matti Niemi and a few other Finns. Although the men received military training, the Civil War concluded in April 1865 before they experienced combat.[16]

Lahti filed an official homestead application in May 1866. His 1871 proof reported that he had thirty-seven acres of land under cultivation; had constructed a sod-roofed house, a chicken coop, and a pigpen; had dug a well; and had planted several apple and shade trees. Some of this accomplished outdoorsman's feats—such as trapping nine thousand muskrats in one year—became part of local legend.[17]

When other Finns arrived in Franklin, the village that served the nearby farming area, some worked for Lahti and his son Charles, which allowed them to pay for their transatlantic passage or earn money for farmland purchases. A boardinghouse, sauna, and several small log cabins, identified as "Finntown" by non-Finns, provided the new arrivals with temporary quarters. The Franklin enclave was among the first of many Finntowns that emerged elsewhere in Minnesota and North America. Renville County's Finnish immigrant population crested at 155 in 1895.[18]

The state's second rural Finnish community developed in Wright County at Cokato (originally Mooers Prairie), settled in 1858 by Swedes, including several from Värmland. The first Finn was Isaac Hare (Haara), who filed a homestead entry in February 1865 while serving with the Union Army; when Hare's wife died within a year, he departed and was never heard from again. Later in 1865 four other Finns arrived from Norway: Mathias Kärjenaho, Elias Peltoperä, Johan Viinikka, and Olaf Westerberg. (The first three were born in northern Finland; Westerberg was a Värmland Finn.) The men walked fifty miles from Minneapolis to Wright County's "Big Woods," where they staked out eighty-acre homesteads but made no improvements until 1866.[19]

One of Franklin's abandoned nineteenth-century Finntown log buildings, 1977.

Additional Finns arrived as word of Cokato's agricultural attributes spread to northern Finland, Norway, and Sweden and to Michigan's "Copper Country." No other rural Minnesota community would be populated by so many Finns from Sweden and Norway. Arriving in 1867 from a Finnish community on the Swedish side of the Tornio valley were Isak and Eva Barberg (Parpa). While Barberg hoped to work as a tailor in Minneapolis, his wife insisted on a rural life. "I won't leave my house," she exclaimed, "I prefer the forest to the city." Some years later the Barberg's homestead proof noted that their one-story house, with its single door and six windows, was "comfortable . . . to live in."[20]

By 1870 only twenty immigrant Finns resided in Cokato Township, but almost seventy-five families joined them over the next ten years. Now, however, many had to search for farmland in nearby areas—north of Cokato in French Lake Township, farther northeast by Annandale in Albion and Corinna townships, and west in the Meeker County townships of Dassel and Kingston.[21]

Temperance Corner in rural Cokato is named for the *Onnen Toivo* (Hope for Happiness) Temperance Society hall, located in the background of this early-twentieth-century photograph. The 1896 hall, now a community center and listed in the National Register of Historic Places in 1976, is the only original structure still remaining at Temperance Corner, although several other historic buildings have been moved to the site, including America's oldest sauna.

In 1879, Barberg compiled the first census of Finns in the greater Cokato area—now an expanse thirty-five by fifty miles in size. Barberg, also a Lutheran lay pastor, determined that 400 of all 450 immigrants resided on farms; they had cleared 1,500 acres of land; owned 43 horses, 121 oxen, and 200 cows; and had holdings valued at $105,000. With a male-female ratio of six to five by 1880, the Cokato area had already assumed the social characteristics of a mature farming community. The combined Finnish immigrant population of Wright and Meeker counties reached its apex of 660 in 1920.[22]

Holmes City, Minnesota's third rural Finnish settlement, served the Douglas County townships of Moe, Holmes City, and Urness. Nine Finns, all of whom came from northern Norway, arrived in late 1866: Peter and Kreeta Julin and their four children, and three single men—Isak Johnson, August Peteri, and Johan Piippo. Three adults were born in Finland, two in Sweden.[23]

After a brief period in Red Wing, the Finns "decided to go and look" at Douglas County, a place where "free land was available in the wilderness." The men selected their homesteads from a map in the St. Cloud land office and then hired a "Yankee" land locator to lead them on the eighty-mile-long journey to their properties. With the men walking beside the oxcart that held Kreeta Julin and her children, the group encountered periodic rain and swirling sleet during the two-week trek, which Piippo described "as slow as lice in tar." All nine Finns spent the winter in a quickly constructed sod shanty heated by a fieldstone stove.[24]

Spring's arrival allowed the men to clear some trees and brush from their landholdings, to plant a few crops, and to construct buildings. In 1871, the Julin farm boasted a two-story log house, a large stable, a granary with a straw-thatched roof, and a well; forty of the 160 acres were fenced, with twenty under cultivation. Other Douglas County Finns would succeed as farmers, but the immigrant population remained small, totaling only seventy-one by 1879 and never exceeding 120 thereafter.[25]

Johan Piippo: "An Unusually Large, Healthy, and Powerful Man"

Johan Piippo moved from Finland to Norway in 1862 and immigrated to Michigan in 1864; two years later Piippo was in Red Wing, where he survived a severe bout of cholera. After moving to Holmes City in late 1866, Piippo constructed a log cabin and planted an acre of wheat that was promptly eaten by blue jays. Eventually, however, he sold enough wolf skins to purchase a cow and two oxen—but then his cabin burned to the ground, claiming most of his belongings.

Piippo prevailed, and in 1875 he married Mary Välimaa, the daughter of another Finnish homesteader. Later they divorced, remarried, and divorced again. Piippo then advertised for a bride in Finland; Anna Kaisanen accepted, and the couple married in 1892. Described as "an unusually large, healthy, and powerful man," Piippo was noted for his healing therapies, survival skills, and long treks to hunting, trapping, and fishing sites. Piippo's farm, established in the 1860s and now maintained by a step-great-grandson, is America's longest-lived Finnish dairy operation run continuously by members of the same family.[iii]

Wedding photograph of Johan Piippo and Anna Kaisanen, 1892.

A Minneapolis Finntown

Minneapolis served as the first urban center for Minnesota's Finns. Early immigrants often paused in Minneapolis before moving westward in their search for farmland or employment, and some farmers pursued seasonal work in the city. Minneapolis also was where Finns from the countryside could "spread their wings." Probably because Minneapolis was Minnesota's western gateway to land and jobs, the city served as a more important center for Finns than did St. Paul, its adjacent twin to the east.[26]

Only four Minneapolis residents listed Finland as their place of birth in 1870. The count rose to 49 (36 males, 13 females) in 1880. A few men resided in "shanties," and just two were married; 28 worked as laborers, seven as brick makers, three as "hucksters" (peddlers), and one as a ticket agent. The eleven unmarried females included six maids, four hotel servants, and one boardinghouse keeper. As more Finns arrived, the logical results were noted by the local *Uusi Kotimaa*—established in 1881 as Minnesota's first Finnish-language newspaper: "every so often there is another wedding" wrote a correspondent.[27]

In 1882, four years after starting work at a Shingle Creek brickyard in northwestern Minneapolis, one Finn described it as a "profitable workplace" that offered $1.75 per day and significant overtime opportunities. Nevertheless, the city's erratic employment situation often posed problems for men, although women had little difficulty finding positions as maids and servants. A late-nineteenth-century journalist from Finland commented approvingly about the daughters "of well-to-do [Finnish] farmers who neither fear hard work nor regard domestic labor as shameful." Furthermore, wrote another Minneapolis observer, any unmarried Finnish man desiring a wife "should come here."[28]

The Finnish immigrant population of Minneapolis grew to 353 by 1900. Included among the 177 employed males were 90 laborers, 29 tailors, 18 carpenters and painters, 12 brick makers, eight blacksmiths and metalworkers, seven professionals and supervisors, six proprietors and salesmen, and two shoemakers. The 68 employed single females included 65 servants and domestics, two seamstresses, and one "shoesticher"; only two married females worked outside their homes—as a washerwoman and a "tailoress"—but many accommodated one to eight boarders and roomers in their homes.[29]

Minneapolis reportedly was a "paradise" for Finns who owned businesses, with their first ventures appearing along Washington Avenue and nearby streets. Victor and Ida Newman established a boardinghouse shortly after their 1881 marriage and later opened the Newman Hotel at 214 Washington Avenue North, which housed thirty-four boarders and lodgers in 1900. During the late 1890s, a few Finns began moving to the Humboldt Avenue area, and they dedicated their Apostolic Lutheran church in 1902; the neighborhood quickly became the nucleus for the "Finnish residential center of Minneapolis." A cohesive Finntown of wooden vernacular dwellings, most built by Finnish carpenters, eventually emerged within a zone bordered by Penn Avenue on the west, Girard Avenue to the east, Bassett Creek on the south, and Western Avenue (now Glenwood) to the north.[30]

The earliest business established in Finntown was Isaac (Kauvosaari) Anderson's Humboldt Avenue grocery store, which he moved from North Fourth Street in 1900. Over the following years, more businesses and services sprang up along Western Avenue, and a Socialist workers' hall appeared close to the Lutheran church; two public saunas, one in the Wells Settlement House, were nearby, and Glenwood (now Theodore Wirth) Park served as a venue for outdoor events. Many Finntown women worked for the Northwest Knitting Company (later Munsingwear), which operated a nearby clothing-manufacturing plant from 1904 to 1981.[31]

SIRENIN KASSUN RUOKALA
1411 Glenwood Avenue,
MINNEAPOLIS, MINNESOTA
— Puhelin: Hy. 9792 —

J. KOSKEN
RUOKATAVARA JA TUPAKKA KAUPPA
274 Humboldt Ave. No.,
MINNEAPOLIS, MINNESOTA
— Puhelin: Hy 9796 —

Otto's Meat Market
LIHAKAUPPA
— Ajamme kotiin —
1416 Glenwood Ave., Minneapolis.
— Puhelin: Hy. 0259 —

Minnie Wuokila BARBER SHOP
~ Toivon yleisön kannatusta ~
1610 Glenwood Ave., Minneapolis.

GLENWOOD CAFE
MR. ja MRS. OSTMAN, omist.
Parhaimman laadun ruoka ja palvelua.
Kokeilkaa meidän tuoretta keitettyä
"CHICKEN CHOW MEIN"
1407 Glenwood Ave., Minneapolis.
— Puhelin: Hyland 7925. —

SAUNA
1409 Glenwood Ave.,
Minneapolis, Minn.
Puhelin: Hy. 9998.
HIEROJA JOS HALUTAAN.
Auki: Tiist., Keskiv., Perj. ja Lauant.
Tunnit: kello 1—12 j. pp.

HOME BAKERY
Jacob Pakonen, omist.
AINA SAATAVANA TUOREITA LEIVOKSIA.
1418 Glenwood Ave., Minneapolis
Puhelin: CH. 5113

J. A. KOSKI
Pure Oil Service Station

1421 Glenwood Ave.,
MINNEAPOLIS, MINNESOTA.

ARVID HILTUNEN
Parturi
HYVÄ TYÖ JA KOHTELU.
1406 Glenwood Ave.,
MINNEAPOLIS, MINNESOTA

The Finnish immigrant community of Minneapolis grew steadily, expanding to 875 in 1910, to 1,120 in 1920, and then to 1,155 in 1930. The Minneapolis Finntown was a lively place that also attracted second- and third-generation Finns, but many residents began dispersing to other areas of the Twin Cities following World War II.

New York Mills and West-Central Minnesota

While Cokato served as America's foremost Finnish agricultural settlement into the 1880s, another community soon replaced it: New York Mills. This area of Otter Tail County became a magnet for Finns after the first settlers, Antti and Elsa Puuperä and Tuomas and Maria Autio, arrived in 1874. The two families were members of a contingent of 110 Finns recruited by the Northern Pacific Railroad to Duluth in late 1873. When no employment opportunities were available during the nationwide financial panic of 1873–78, they moved to Brainerd, where the men worked as lumberjacks.[32]

In 1875, after the men's Swedish coworkers informed them about free land in Otter Tail County, the two families settled on homesteads located six miles south of New York Mills (later named Heinola). Over the next forty years more than one thousand Finnish farmers would settle in Newton, Leaf Lake, Deer Creek, Paddock, and Blowers townships, while New York Mills served as an important Finnish American newspaper publication center from 1885 to 1980.[33]

Finns participated wholeheartedly in converting forests into farms, something they were well equipped to perform. "Someone who has toiled in the deep backwoods of Finland," wrote local journalist J. W. Lähde in 1887, "has no fear of the forest." Lähde believed that once the land was cleared of maples, oaks, cedars, and pines its agricultural productivity would equal areas of Finland where "silver-bearded firs" predominated. And, unlike the closely spaced farm buildings of the "old country," the area's two hundred farmsteads revealed a more dispersed pattern. In 1922, another writer recalled the backbreaking work undertaken by Finnish women who had transformed the "deep forest" into agricultural fields: "With an axe, a grub hoe, and a scythe they worked year after year clearing land," he wrote,

New York Mills
has been an
important center
for Minnesota's
Finns since the
mid-1880s.
Thousands of
people from
throughout the
Midwest attended
a June 1934
Midsummer
festival
(*Juhanusjuhla*)
there.

and often proved themselves superior to men when performing this task. Unfortunately, the women died before seeing the "marvelous" results of their efforts.[34]

By 1882 Finns were establishing farms north of New York Mills in Becker County, primarily in the townships of Wolf Lake or *Susijärvi* (the only official Minnesota place name translated into English from Finnish), Green Valley, Spruce Grove, and Runeberg, and to a lesser extent in Carsonville, Toad Lake, and Shell Lake. Finns also developed an important agricultural district east of New York Mills

A large group of men and boys view a new 1912 Case tractor and threshing rig displayed in front of the Sebeka Mercantile Company, founded during the early 1900s by Andrew Helppie, a Finnish immigrant of Sámi descent. Helppie's brother-in-law, Oscar (Niemi) Johnson, also operated a branch of the Sebeka Mercantile in Nashwauk, on the Iron Range.

in five Wadena County townships—Red Eye, Blueberry, Shell River, Rockwood, and Meadow—served by the railroad villages of Menahga and Sebeka from the early 1890s onward.

Runeberg's Finns succeeded in having their township named for Finland's nineteenth-century national poet; elsewhere in Becker County, the small settlement of Snellman and a now-vanished post office at Lonnrot, along with the abandoned railroad stop of Topelius in Otter Tail County, commemorated three other noted men in Finland's national awakening movement. Today, many people identify the New York Mills–Sebeka–Menahga–Wolf Lake district as the "Finnish Triangle"—described by musician Kip Peltoniemi as "the center of the eastern section of the western part of the southern portion of northern Minnesota."[35]

Snellman is typical of small Minnesota hamlets found in many areas of rural Finnish settlement. Since the early 1890s, Snellman has supported a cooperative store and creamery, a private grocery, a tavern, an automobile service station, a dance hall once used as a Finnish Pentecostal church, and the Comet Skiway. Still prominent in 1975 was the Finnish National Evangelical Lutheran church, dedicated in 1913 and razed in 1977 when a new church, Gethsemane Lutheran, was built nearby.

Northeastern Minnesota: Duluth, Rural Settlements, Timber Camps, Mill and Mining Towns

No more than 130 Finns resided in northeastern Minnesota by 1880. A token number had settled in Duluth during the late 1860s, while the subsequent decade saw some movement to Brainerd and to two rural townships just west of Duluth. Northeastern Minnesota would not become the state's primary Finnish settlement region until the late 1880s and early 1890s, a time when immigrants began pursuing work in Duluth, in timber camps, in mill and mining towns, and on hardscrabble farms.[36]

Duluth: "The Helsinki of America"

The first Finns appeared in Duluth in 1868, but according to one chronicler, "they did not settle down in that little disorderly town." There is some evidence that in 1869 fisherman Johan Moilanen became Duluth's first Finnish resident; only seven Finns, six of them fishermen, followed him over the next three years. Because of Duluth's location—at the head of Lake Superior and about halfway between the Finnish mining communities of Michigan and the rural settlements of Minnesota—the city initially served as a transfer point for Finns. Apparently none of the Finns recruited by the Northern Pacific Railroad in 1873 made Duluth a permanent home, and only nine Finnish men resided there two years later.[37]

The emergence of northeastern Minnesota's late-nineteenth-century timber and iron ore industries led to Duluth's growing importance as a sawmilling, wholesale trade, shipping, and transportation center. Its population grew from 3,485 in 1880 to 52,970 in 1900 and then to 98,915 in 1920. The Finnish presence also expanded noticeably, increasing from 415 in 1885 to 705 in 1900 and to 2,770 in 1910 before peaking at 3,120 in 1920. Males formed just over 75 percent of Duluth's Finnish population in 1885; the figures declined slowly to 70 percent in 1900, to 65 percent in 1910, and to 63 percent in 1920. The size of the Finnish community, however, fluctuated with the seasons. During temperate months, men found employment as dock and sawmill workers or engaged in the construction of buildings, roads, railroads, and utility lines. When these jobs ended with winter's arrival, many laid-off laborers headed for the region's timber camps.[38]

While a late-nineteenth-century Finnish writer claimed Duluth's Finns were in "a wretched state of moral decay, the like of which is hardly to be found elsewhere," the *Duluth Evening Herald* offered a much more upbeat assessment. "The Finns are generally intelligent and patriotic," reported the newspaper in 1900, "they are hardy and industrious" and, moreover, "they make good citizens and an increase in their numbers will be welcomed." The reasons for these contradictory perceptions reflect the predominance of young unmarried men in the population, the shortage of social and cultural opportunities, and, as will be described later, the political divisions between conservative and radical Finns.[39]

Duluth's first Finnish fishermen resided in squatters' shanties situated on a low area of land at the northern end of Minnesota Point—a sandy peninsula that protects the city's harbor from Lake Superior's winds and storms. During the 1880s, the settlement locus shifted slightly to St. Croix Avenue (now Canal Park Drive). To Finns, the four-block-long avenue was *Rottakatu* ("Rat Street"), a name that likely described the noticeable presence of rodents, whereas English-language newspapers occasionally referred to "Finlander Avenue."[40]

By 1910, some 1,120 people were crowded into St. Croix Avenue's boardinghouses and multi-unit residences; 810 were Finnish immigrants and another 130 their American-born children. The entire group of 940 constituted 85 percent of the avenue's population—undoubtedly the densest concentration of Finns ever seen in the Midwest. In fact,

More than nine hundred Finns and their children were packed into the boardinghouses, rooming houses, and apartments of Duluth's St. Croix Avenue district during the early 1900s.

fire insurance maps identified the St. Croix Avenue area as a "congested district" by 1908. In 1911, Finnish resident Abel Salo claimed it was impossible to find fresh air anywhere along the avenue.[41]

The crowded conditions and noise generated by St. Croix's public saunas and "soup shops" were also upsetting to Salo. The disgruntled Finn claimed the nightly "clatter" didn't even allow one to think of sleep. "But why should peace for a worker matter," asked Salo sarcastically, "when businessmen are in such a rush to make money?"[42]

The avenue's 1910 population of foreign-born Finns included 635 males and 155 females—almost a four-to-one ratio. Only 84 (13 percent) of adult males were married. Of the 155 adult females, 86 (55 percent) were married and 60 were single, including eight widows. The unmarried women worked in boardinghouses, hotels, and restaurants as servants, dishwashers, or cooks; and just two married women worked outside their homes, although "home" for 51 of the 84 households meant that boarders and lodgers also lived in the residential unit.[43]

Boardinghouse conditions varied considerably, but the rooming house situation was often deplorable. In 1913, a two-room unit in one West Second Street rooming house included seventeen Finns—a husband and wife, a recent widow, and fourteen children, two with smallpox. Another rooming house, situated above a St. Croix Avenue lunch-room, had dirty bunk beds crowded into tiny quarters; the third-floor attic, where one could barely stand because of the steep roof angle, received limited light and ventilation through a pair of diminutive openings. Another room was occupied throughout the night by a noisy "poker gang," while the preaching and "righteous" songs of a Finnish gospel meeting emanated from an adjoining building.[44]

Boardinghouses

Duluth's first Finnish boardinghouse or *poikatalo* appeared in 1881, and many others emerged thereafter. By the early twentieth century, any urban place populated by significant numbers of unmarried male Finns had at least one Finnish boardinghouse. In addition, Finnish family homes often housed three to ten boarders, but some had twenty-five or more. Cooperative boardinghouses were also established by Finns in Duluth, Cloquet, International Falls, Brainerd, Minneapolis, and most Iron Range towns. These nonprofit ventures offered lower rates than privately operated facilities and provided patrons with familiar and higher-quality food. In 1926, a total of twenty-four Finnish cooperative boardinghouses remained in Minnesota.

Duluth Finnish consul and businessman Alex Kyyhkynen noted that because of the board-inghouses "there was no incentive for the men to get married. Life was too comfortable. Most of them died bachelors." After the last Finnish boardinghouses closed during the 1950s, these aging bachelors spent their final years in inexpensive hotels and rooming houses and on county poor farms. Following their deaths, the brief obituaries often concluded with a poignant statement: "there are no known survivors."[iv]

Several members and two female employees of the Toverila Cooperative Boardinghouse stand outside their building on Superior Street in Duluth, c. 1920. With a membership of 338 in 1926, Toverila was Minnesota's largest Finnish cooperative boardinghouse; Cloquet's Toivola had 280 members.

Other multi-unit facilities with Finnish inhabitants extended to Lake Avenue and nearby streets by the mid-1880s. While the greater St. Croix Avenue area remained a residential stronghold for Finns until the 1960s, some émigrés were already settling in West Duluth during the 1880s. Other than several Finnish maids, only a few affluent Finns resided in the wealthier neighborhoods of eastern Duluth.[45]

Johan Rento's St. Croix Avenue tailor shop opened in 1884, while Victor Lauri's *Suomlainen Salooni* ("Finnish Saloon"), a Lake Avenue attraction, emerged one year later. Duluth's first public saunas soon appeared (at least ten operated by 1914), as did Harry and Mary Hill's St. Croix Avenue store, with an adjacent boardinghouse. (One son operated the store into the 1960s.) Finnish shoemakers, plumbers,

Finnish immigrant women performed endless chores on their farms, including Emma Vähätalo Alanen of Snellman, shown here pumping water for the family's cows on a cold winter day during the early 1920s.

seventy-five hours, although some toiled one hundred hours. Elsewhere, Cloquet had thirty female servants; 110 inhabited smaller towns and farms.

While the daughters of Finnish immigrants were more likely to fill factory, clerical, and professional positions, some also worked as domestics. When Alma Siiro Lunden (Lundeen) left her family's remote Aitkin County farm to attend Duluth's Central High School during the early 1920s, she earned room and board as a live-in domestic, which sometimes offered less-than-ideal conditions. In one home she wasn't allowed to eat the same food as the family and her room "was bare, except for a sagging bed and a wooden apple box for my clothes and other things"; on another occasion "an instinct for self-preservation," which she attributed to "growing up in the wilderness," allowed her to flee the advances of a predatory landlord. Only small numbers of Finns immigrated to Minnesota after World War II, but young women such as Helmi Pursiainen could still find work as maids. The Kuopio resident moved to Sweden during the early 1950s, some years after the deaths of her only sibling, a sixteen-year-old brother killed in the Finnish-Soviet War, and her parents. In 1956 she immigrated to Duluth and was soon hired by a wealthy East Side Jewish family; she subsequently moved to Los Angeles, married, and became a U.S. citizen.[v]

carpenters, bakers, restaurateurs, jewelers, clothiers, midwives, masseuses, billiard and tobacco shop operators, seamstresses, chauffeurs, teamsters, and soda pop distributors augmented the immigrant community by the early 1900s. Now it was possible for Duluth's Finns to conduct most of their daily transactions in a familiar language.[46]

Journalists, Lutheran ministers, lawyers, dentists, and physicians—including Dr. Y. I. Lindgren, who opened his twenty-bed National Hospital at 1427 East First Street in 1914—formed the coterie of Finnish professionals. Lindgren's "knife skills" were so exceptional, claimed one tongue-in-cheek account, that no Finn should fear his surgical "stabs." Walk-in patients consulted with the popular doctor at his downtown office, where he dispensed advice and prescriptions for "elixirs" that treated illnesses ranging from nervous disorders and weak blood to rheumatism and constipation. Ten years later Drs. Onne and Ida Jurva arrived from Menahga to establish a naturopathic and chiropractic clinic they operated for three decades.[47]

Duluth's Finns formed their first organization in 1881, a short-lived cultural society, while a band, temperance society, and Lutheran congregation emerged later in the decade. The flowering of Finnish organizations occurred from the 1890s to the early 1940s, when political, athletic, theatrical, and musical groups proliferated, as did literary and debate clubs, and additional religious congregations. Most impressive were a college for workers and numerous newspapers and periodicals published in the city. Early-morning Finnish-language news and religious radio broadcasts could also be heard on two Duluth stations during the 1930s and 1940s, a practice that led to some complaints: "from 6:30-7:00 A.M. . . . we might as well be in Finland or in church," wrote one non-Finnish critic. No wonder that former president Herbert Hoover, during a late-1939 stop in Duluth, acknowledged that he was in "the Finnish capital of the United States."[48]

Logging Camps and Mill Towns

Because of previous experiences in their homeland, many Finnish men were well prepared to work in the timber industry. As Ojibwe elder Paul Buffalo observed, forest work was something "Finlanders are really good at." Untold numbers of Finns toiled as lumberjacks in northeastern Minnesota's logging camps from the 1890s through the 1930s. The jacks' season stretched from September into May, although most work occurred during the winter months. Large firms such as the Virginia and Rainy Lake Company, which had 145 camps that employed up to 2,800 men annually, hired numerous Finns; some men, however, elected to work in smaller facilities operated by their Finnish compatriots. No matter where they found employment, the hazardous nature of the lumberjacks' work was exacerbated by isolation, a lack of medical services, and deplorable living conditions.[49]

Lumberjacks performed various jobs in the woods. "Notchers" marked trees for cutting, while "sawyers" felled them with two-man saws. After "swampers" cleared the logging trails that were frozen and maintained by "road monkeys," the "skidders" drove horses that towed the logs to rail and river landings where loading crews congregated. When water was nearby, "river rats" engaged in a dangerous springtime ritual: floating the logs to a mill. The camp headquarters, another male domain, included the foreman, clerk, barn boss, blacksmiths, saw filers, teamsters, and cooks. Finnish-owned camps often had female cooks who provided familiar ethnic foods such as *viili* (curdled milk), hardtack, and fruit soup and used butter rather than margarine.[50]

A Finnish camp was always distinguished by its sauna, where lumberjacks bathed regularly to rid themselves of lice, fleas, and bedbugs. Some non-Finnish camps also had saunas constructed of timber and stone by lumberjacks

A female cook was employed in this early-twentieth-century Finnish lumber camp, located in northeastern Minnesota.

during free-time hours. Since the sauna was the only camp building not under company control, it symbolized the Finns' ability to attain "some social power in an environment of domination."[51]

Some non-Finnish lumberjacks (especially South Slavs) eagerly used the saunas, although the folklore associated with camp life also described the plight of reluctant or uninformed participants, such as an Irishman who "kicked and screamed and hollered" when the Finns pulled off his clothes and cleaned and parboiled him on the sauna's top bench. After carrying the Irishman outside for cooling, the Finns discovered that "underneath the clothes they had stripped off of him ... [was] last winter's underwear."[52]

All Minnesota timber towns had districts that catered to lumberjacks who sought excitement and opportunities "to go on a binge" after spending time in the pineries. Arthur Kylländer, a popular Finnish songwriter and performer whose lyrics "combined humor with a biting social commentary," noted the attractions of these places in his 1927 song "Lumberjäkki":

> We have only one life to live
> Guys, let's go and celebrate in the city.[53]

Cloquet, which emerged as Carlton County's largest Finnish center during the 1890s, was widely known for the "colorful doings" of lumberjacks who congregated on Dunlap Island. But to writer Walter O'Meara, who grew up in the turn-of-the-century town, Cloquet offered something more: it was also "filled with wonders and marvels," such as friends who spoke English, Finnish, Swedish, and Ojibwe. The Finntown where many of O'Meara's friends lived was "distinguished by a huge frame boardinghouse, a community sauna, and houses painted in vivid shades of pink, green, blue, and mauve—people called them Finlander colors."[54]

Sawmills, including major facilities in Cloquet, Duluth, Winton, and especially Virginia, where the Virginia and Rainy Lake Company ran the world's largest white pine mill from 1909 to 1929, also provided employment. Companies that built pulp and paper mills in Cloquet, Brainerd, Grand Rapids, and International Falls during the late nineteenth and early twentieth centuries—and later opened factories for the manufacture of toothpicks, matches, and wallboard— offered work for both men and women. Eventually it became commonplace for many northeastern Minnesota Finns to say proudly, "I work at the mill."[55]

Iron Range

No section of Minnesota has been more heavily populated and affected by Finns than the Iron Range, a district that provided, for the first half of the twentieth century, 70 percent of the nation's and almost 25 percent of the world's iron ore output. Three "ranges" define Minnesota's mining district: the Vermilion, which shipped its first iron ore in 1884; the gigantic Mesabi, where shipments commenced in 1892; and the Cuyuna, which began exporting ore in 1911. The Cuyuna's deposits were actually discovered by Finnish immigrant Henry Pajari in 1882 when the experienced miner was traveling by train from Michigan to his New York Mills homestead. Noticing similarities between the rock formations of the Upper Peninsula's Marquette range and eastern Crow Wing County, Pajari subsequently spent several months excavating for ore, but a shortage of capital ended his dreams of fortune.[56]

Early mining communities were raw and austere places. In 1903, Virginia's main street was described as replete with "rottenness and filth," while the "stench" emitting from Hibbing was caused by "heaps of filth [that] lie everywhere in the alleys and door yards and even in the public thoroughfares." Eveleth teacher Polly Bullard described one public sauna as "a high unpainted barn-like building with few windows" that emitted, each Saturday evening, "a frequent stream of bathwater draining out at the bottom and over the sidewalk into the gutter." When Liisa Ranta-Aho arrived in early-twentieth-century Eveleth, the young Finnish woman expressed great disappointment over the two feet of mud flanking the boardwalks. "This is a heck of a place to bring me, compared to the rosy picture I have painted of it on my way up here," she complained to her new husband. Conditions improved after World War I, when generous tax revenues generated by the range's vast ore reserves allowed local municipalities to develop an outstanding array of schools, public buildings, and services seldom equaled in other places of similar size in America.[57]

Just nineteen Finnish immigrants lived on the Vermilion in 1885, but by 1895 the 955 Finns comprised its largest foreign-born group, as they did in 1905 when their numbers reached 1,510. The Mesabi, however, became their principal domain: the Finns' total Iron Range numbers increased from 4,410 in 1900 to 8,310 in 1910 and then to 9,325 in 1920. At times, Finns formed up to 40 percent of the entire foreign-born population.[58]

Most Iron Range communities were characterized by a sizable, if not dominant, Finnish presence. Virginia, with 1,605 Finns in 1920, was the foremost Mesabi center, followed by Hibbing (1,450), Chisholm (890), Eveleth (670), Aurora (560), Nashwauk (530), and Gilbert (490). Ely (380) led the Vermilion, Crosby (360) the Cuyuna.[59]

Males formed 82 percent of the Iron Range Finnish population in 1895; the figure declined to 71 percent in 1900 and then to 60 percent in 1920. In 1902, Minnesota's commissioner of labor reported that 40 percent of Minnesota's seven to eight thousand mining employees were Finns—men he described as "strong, well-built, used to hard work and meager fare." Three years later almost 37 percent of Finnish men in Eveleth worked as miners; another 53 percent were "day

Legends and Folklore: From Glass Eaters to "Knife Hooligans"

Finnish communities typically included at least one person whose exploits or appearance became part of local folklore. One was Matt Ilka of Kinney, who, in 1899, endeavored "to startle the natives" of the Iron Range by eating beer glasses. An active glass eater in 1941 at age sixty-two, Ilka still claimed "robust health" and "unusually strong" teeth. Elsewhere, in Aitkin County's Salo Township, two bachelors, both of whom changed their names to Charles (Kalle) Anderson, were renowned for the poor quality of their clothing; one was identified as *Resu-Kalle* ("Ragged Charley"), whereas the other was termed *Parempi-Kalle* ("Better Charley")—only because of his slightly improved garb. In Esko, Mary Winter, who performed characteristically men's work, called herself "Pants Mary" because she wore trousers under her dress, an unusual practice among early-twentieth-century women.

Otto Walta's reputation extended beyond his northern St. Louis County home in Idington. Termed "hard as nails and tough as a bull moose," Walta was deemed capable of ripping "good-sized trees right out of the ground" and able to wield a thirty-foot-long tamarack pole when prying up pine stumps. A prodigious eater who once inadvertently consumed all the food prepared for a large family, Walta reportedly could eat washtub-size loaves of bread and drink all the milk in a three-gallon pail with one gulp.

Walta apparently spent a rowdy youth in Finland, but the immigrant bachelor's Minnesota years were distinguished by a respect for people, animals, and even the bedbugs that inhabited his mattress. Choosing to pull his plow rather than burdening a horse, Walta secured traction by fabricating a pair of shoes that replaced the soles and heels with pieces of plate iron that had spikes bolted to them. In 1942, after a neighbor claimed Walta suffered from "fever and hallucinations," he was committed to the state hospital in Moose Lake, living there for sixteen years until his death at age eighty-two.

Some of Minnesota's Finnish communities had one or more "knife hooligans" (*puukojunkarit*)—a term that originally described young males who disrupted celebrations in rural Ostrobothnia. Duluth and Iron Range newspapers included embellished accounts of

Finns who "carved" their compatriots "just by way of amusement" and described their conflicts, often with Italians, "as mass[es] of heads, hands, feet and teeth." Because of the "actions of a few," however, Finnish men in general could also find themselves identified "as incorrigible, sometimes brutal drunks."[vi]

Folk legend Otto Walta, second from right, with four other lumberjacks in northeastern Minnesota.

David Schibel, a member of Finland's small Jewish community, immigrated to America in 1902 and operated a Virginia clothing store in partnership with Gust Singer from 1909 to 1933; Schibel's son Howard then joined his father in operating the Palace Clothing Company. This Finnish-language advertisement is headlined, "Fellow citizens. Notice the Helsinki boy's clothing store."

laborers," men who removed the glacial overburden covering the ore deposits or toiled as timbermen, teamsters, and unskilled workers; the remaining 10 percent were carpenters, tailors, shoemakers, clerks, merchants, and saloonkeepers. Small numbers of professional men were found in some cities; one, the prominent Socialist leader Dr. Antero Tanner, opened an early-twentieth-century hospital in Ely and later moved to Chisholm. During the late nineteenth and early twentieth centuries, most unmarried Finnish women worked as servants, primarily in boardinghouses. Only a few married women worked outside their homes, but many provided room and board for single men.[60]

The dangers associated with mining were spelled out in a distressing toll of deaths and injuries. Death was so commonplace that early English-language newspapers seldom provided the names of unmarried victims; instead, the deceased was identified only as "a Finn," "an Italian," or "a Slav." Apparently the first Finnish fatality was an anonymous miner killed by falling rocks and ore in 1884: "His body was crushed beyond any semblance to human form," reported Tower's newspaper, "and his remains were brought up the shaft in a gunnysack." When another Vermilion miner plunged to his death while clearing a clogged ore chute in 1893, the editor, ever ready to offer caustic comments about Finns, claimed the death was similar to "a man who sat on the limb of a tree while he sawed it off."[61]

When married men died, their families faced immediate financial devastation. Peter Lassila, killed at Aurora's Auburn mine in 1897, was survived by his widow and three children in Finland, whereas Matt Erickson, who died of a broken back and crushed skull in the Hull mine near

Hibbing, left his widow and three young offspring "in destitute circumstances." Following fifty-eight hours of entombment in the Commodore mine in 1897, Elias Pekkala vowed never again to work as a miner. "The solitude of that cold chamber was something terrible, and I cannot begin to tell you one-half of the horrors I endured," recounted Pekkala. "Only those who have had death, long drawn out, staring them in the face, can realize what I suffered."[62]

Two years after his 1903 election to the Minnesota House of Representatives, Finnish immigrant John Saari sponsored a bill calling for improved safety measures and accurate counts of mining accidents and deaths. Following its passage, the state mining inspector reported that a record 177 deaths had occurred in Iron Range mines from mid-1905 through mid-1907; the seventy-seven Finns represented the largest ethnic group. Despite this carnage, the inspector still maintained the official line—namely, that most deaths were due to the victims' carelessness or heedlessness. Conditions improved after World War I, but the forty-two deaths (eight of them Finns) caused by the 1924 flooding of the Cuyuna's Milford mine remains the worst mining accident in Minnesota history. Altogether, more than three hundred Finns perished in Minnesota's mines from 1884 to 1930, and untold numbers died of mine-related injuries or illnesses.[63]

Farming the Cutover

The dangers of mining, coupled with employment fluctuations, periodic strikes, and the discriminatory attitudes of company officials, led many Finns to flee the range and establish farms in the cutover region—a vast section of northeastern Minnesota, northern Wisconsin, and upper Michigan that remained in a "cutover" state after its extensive tree cover was removed by loggers. Joining the displaced miners were thousands of other Finns who came from timber camps, cities, and Finland itself. Between 1884 and 1922, as Finns established themselves in more than fifty rural settlements throughout northeastern Minnesota, many men still worked part time as miners and lumberjacks to supplement their often meager farm income.[64]

During the early 1870s, small numbers of homesteaders entered two adjacent townships west of Duluth: Midway (St. Louis County) and Thomson (Carlton County). In 1872, Kalle and Eva Kytömäki (Hendrickson) became the first Finns to file a homestead claim in Midway (Fond du Lac until 1898)—described as a place of "backwoods and bears"; sixty Finns lived there by 1880. During the early settlement years the men often walked ten to fifteen miles to Duluth to seek work and secure supplies. While the Kytömäki's scenic Pine Hill dairy farm became Midway's most successful agricultural venture, it was converted into a nine-hole golf course in 1928; the family managed the course until 2002, when another owner purchased it.[65]

Simeon and Katariina Palkki (Palkie) were among the first of several Finns who established Thomson Township homesteads in 1873; just over fifty Finns had settled there by 1880. Thomson's pioneers developed northeastern Minnesota's initial Finnish cooperative venture in 1878 when they constructed a water-powered gristmill along the Midway River that provided flour for rye bread. Esko's Corner (now Esko) emerged at a Thomson township crossroads in 1890 and soon became one of Minnesota's best-known Finnish settlements.[66]

Other Finnish communities eventually sprang up west and southwest of Midway and Thomson. From 1888 to 1894, Finns began developing a farming district in the Carlton County townships of Kalevala, Automba, Moose Lake, Mahtowa, Silver (Kettle River), Lakeview (Wright), and Eagle and Red Clover (Cromwell). The district also expanded westward into several Aitkin County townships: Salo (Lawler), Beaver, Spalding, Rice River (East Lake), and Clark (Tamarack). One Aitkin County farmer contentedly described his "wonderful home" in 1913, located "far away from the big world, with its...bloodthirsty factories." Southwestern St. Louis County—Floodwood, Cedar Valley, Halden, Prairie Lake, and Van Buren townships—began attracting Finns during the late 1890s, as did Embarrass Township to the north. Finns attempted to settle Allen Township just northeast of Embarrass, but conditions proved so difficult that its subsistence farms and local government were soon abandoned. The earliest of Itasca County's Finnish communities emerged at Trout Lake Township before 1900.[67]

During the 1930s, volunteers began restoring the cooperative gristmill, originally built on Erick Palkki's farm near Esko in 1878. The mill and several historic buildings are now on display in the Esko Historical Society Museum.

The Finns' southernmost rural cutover community appeared in 1894 when the St. Paul and Duluth Railroad started disposing of its Pine County landholdings, located five miles west of Finlayson. Marketed among their fellow Finns by John Oldenberg and J. H. Jasberg, the settlement was named *Nurmijärvi*, also a well-known town in Finland, by the two businessmen. While land agents commonly exaggerated the virtues of places they promoted, Jasberg's approach was tempered by some realism, including his observation that the best potential farmer was "a strong, steady laborer with a large family" and an "industrious wife." Jasberg also cautioned fellow agents "never to sell a farm or cutover farm land to a man whose wife objects moving to the country." Pine County's Finnish immigrant population peaked at 365 in 1905, including a group of quarrymen and their families located outside of Sandstone.[68]

From 1900 to 1922, the state's Finnish settlement mosaic both filled in and expanded, extending beyond the northwestern edge of the cutover to Middle River and Plummer. Again, however, it was rural St. Louis County that drew most Finns. By 1920, the townships and settlements in the county's southern half with more than seventy Finnish residents included Bassett, Cherry, Clinton, Colvin (Markham and nearby Makinen), Fairbanks, Industrial (Saginaw), Lavell, McDavitt (Zim), Toivola, and White (Palo). Farther north were Alango, Angora, Balkan, Leiding (Orr), Pike, Sandy (Britt), Vermilion Lake (Peyla), Waasa, and Wuori (Florenton) townships. After spending the winter of 1932–33 north of the Mesabi, "a place where most farmers would starve," aspiring Minnesota author Glanville Smith surmised that only Finns could "convert muskeg to milk" in such a "cold, rocky, lonesome country."[69]

Split Rock Township and Sawyer were added to Carlton County's Finnish settlements list during the early 1900s, as were Logan (Palisade) and Ball Bluff (Jacobson) townships, both located along the Mississippi River in Aitkin County. When J. W. Lähde made a 1903 visit to Jacobson—known to Finns as *Suomi Siirtola* ("Finnish Settlement")—the journalist claimed its residents were creating "a small picture of their native land." Farming communities also emerged in the Itasca County townships of Balsam and Nashwauk, at Suomi, located by Little Bowstring Lake, and Squaw Lake. Koochiching County's Finnish homesteaders

Around 1917, Olga Bergström Petrell (Peltari) photographed the horse-drawn mower used on the small dairy farm she and her husband, Edwin, established in the St. Louis County township of Fairbanks, north of Brimson; because of the rocky, uneven fields, some hay cutting was still done by men with hand scythes.

initially settled in the Ray-Kabetogama Lake area and later by Ranier, Big Falls, and Little Fork.[70]

Finns also moved into Lake County, first Two Harbors, where dock and railroad work was available by the late nineteenth century, and then to logging-farming settlements at Finland, Isabella, and Toimi. While the swampy and stony Toimi (and nearby Brimson) area posed extreme difficulties for immigrant Finnish farmers, one pioneer woman described their fortitude or *sisu:* her sister, she colorfully wrote, was born "between the rocks and the strawberries." By 1934, three decades after the first Finns arrived, Finland's remaining residents were still attempting to wrest a living from dairy farms that averaged only twenty acres of cleared land. Almost all farming had ended by the late 1940s, but residents found employment at a nearby U.S. Air Force radar station.[71]

Finns and the Fires of 1918

Minnesota's worst disaster occurred over Columbus Day 1918, when massive forest fires destroyed sections of Carlton, St. Louis, and Aitkin counties. More than five hundred people died directly in the inferno—commonly called the Cloquet-Moose Lake fire—and untold numbers later succumbed to injuries or diseases such as Spanish influenza; some took their own lives. The conflagration obviously didn't discriminate among ethnic groups, but Finns suffered disproportionately because so many lived in the burned-over area, especially the Carlton County communities of Cloquet and Kettle River and the townships of Automba, Kalevala, Lakeview, Perch Lake, Progress, Silver, and Thomson. At least 175 Finnish immigrants and their children were killed directly—the greatest loss of life ever experienced by North America's Finns in a single incident. Many were buried in a mass grave, but St. Peter's Lutheran Cemetery by Kettle River offers a painful reminder of the grief encountered by individual families; most touching are the seven small markers on the Koivisto family plot, each marking a child's gravesite.[vii]

Aina Jokimaki, the sixteen-year-old daughter of Finnish immigrants who resided in Carlton County's Silver Township, suffered severe injuries to her feet and legs while walking over burning stumps and trees in the immediate aftermath of the massive 1918 conflagration. Her mother and all six siblings died in the inferno.

Clearing cutover land was an onerous, time-consuming task that demanded the removal of rocks, stumps, and smaller trees passed over by loggers. While homesteaders had some financial advantage over the much larger number who purchased their land, agricultural progress was slow for everyone. Thirty Finns who "proved up" their homesteads in Kalevala and Salo townships between 1888 and 1907 cleared an average of only 1.5 acres of land annually during their initial five to seven years of farming.[72]

Finnish bachelors engaged in farming, and some men worked alone when their wives refused to join them. Atami Kemppainen, a Kalevala Township homesteader, woefully noted in 1898 that his wife had "never been in this country, refuses to come; am being as a widower." (He remarried in 1899.) A few single females attempted farming, but married women could find themselves saddled with endless difficulties and debts if their husbands died prematurely or were incapacitated by illness or injury. One desperate Salo Township woman sent a letter, written in broken English, to "our greatly loved President [Theodore] Roosevelt" in 1905, describing the pitiful situation she and her three young sons faced. The woman wrote that two years earlier her husband was committed to the state hospital when he "came insane." Since he was not a naturalized citizen when institutionalized, the woman was frantic that legal restrictions would make it impossible to "pruve" the homestead. "We have been living on the land since filing and worked on it with all our might," she informed the president. "And now I have thought I would ask you dear sir what could I do so I could get something from the work [that] here is done." The letter concluded with a plea: "I am waiting . . . for a letter from your high person." Fortunately, the government modified its policy and she secured the title in 1906.[73]

Ralph Wilen photographed a Finnish bachelor neighbor (c. 1914) as he worked by his new one-room cabin, located close to the Automba and Salo township boundary (Carlton and Aitkin counties, respectively).

Farmsteads and Buildings

Finnish farmsteads, whether constructed in Finland or Minnesota, revealed certain similarities—particularly the buildings, usually constructed of logs and often grouped around a central open area. While other immigrant groups also erected log structures, Finnish American buildings have been acclaimed for their "carefully hewn, closely fitted" construction and sophisticated examples of "double, full dovetail, or tooth notching."[74]

Since well-established farms in Finland evolved over many generations, farmsteads had as many as twenty-two buildings—considerably more than an incipient northeastern Minnesota enclave with its four to six small structures: house, barn(s), sauna, root cellar, and privy. Minnesota farms that moved beyond the subsistence stage often included an additional three to five of the following buildings: granary, horse stable, well/milk house, summer kitchen, chicken coop, icehouse, smokehouse, smithy, pigsty, garage, woodshed, machine shed, *riihi* (a heated building used for drying grain), and field hay barns. Eventually, northeastern Minnesota's most successful Finnish farms would have twelve to fifteen buildings.[75]

The carefully formed dovetailed notches of the Petrell Hall in northeastern Fairbanks Township still display the skills of the Finnish immigrant builders who crafted them in 1912. The second log from the top at the left is fifteen inches wide.

Since prospective farmers recognized the need for immediate protection from Minnesota's inclement weather, the initial shelter might be a lean-to, hut, or one-room log cabin that could later become the sauna or be expanded into a larger dwelling. Geographer Matti Kaups's surveys (1962–80) of two hundred Finnish log houses in the cutover region revealed that originally almost 20 percent

A one-room cabin on the Aho farm, located north of Chisholm in *Korvenkylä* ("Woodland Village"), served both as a residence and sauna until a larger dwelling was built. Thereafter, the cabin was used only as a smoke sauna (*savusauna*).

were one-room cabins, 50 percent one-story houses with two rooms, and 30 percent one-and-one-half story, two-story, and unique examples.[76]

The simplest barns sheltered a few cows and perhaps a horse and some chickens. Later, when farmers Americanized their barns by building gambrel roofs topped by cupolas, the structures often retained some Finnish features, such as log walls. The *lato,* a field barn used for hay storage, was unique to Finnish farms. Thousands of latos once punctuated the fields of Minnesota's Finnish settlements; only a few remain today.[77]

The sauna has always served as "the sign of the Finn." Until the 1920s, a Minnesota Finnish farm was characterized by its *savusauna* ("smoke sauna"), a chimneyless building heated by a *kiuas*—a stove built of unmortared fieldstone that was fired with wood for four to seven

Members of the Paavola family pose at their Angora Township farmstead during the early 1900s; two examples of a Finnish field hay barn (*lato*) are visible in the background.

An early 1900s two-bay barn on the Gregorius and Mary Hanka farmstead in Embarrass Township is similar to centuries-old examples in Finland. The front bay, with spaces between the logs, was for hay; the rear bay, or "warm barn," with tightly fitted logs, housed the cows; and the central roofed-over space was typically used for flailing grain and storing hay or equipment. The preservation of the Hanka farmstead and several other rural Finnish buildings in the Embarrass area was initiated in 1987 by a local organization, Sisu Heritage, Inc. Also in St. Louis County at Makinen is the Eli Wirtanen Pioneer Farm, where local preservation efforts commenced during the 1970s.

hours. After the fire died down and the smoke and fumes had exited through the open doorway and a vent, the naked sauna-goers entered the well-heated space; there, inside the pitch-black chamber, they threw water on the heated rocks to create *löyly* ("steam") and switched themselves with a small *vihta* or *vasta* made of cedar or birch branches. Some savusaunas also served as maternity rooms and places for administering folk therapies. The Finns' sauna rituals could appear strange and even bizarre to outsiders, some of whom believed that magic and witchcraft were practiced inside the huts. One Esko farmer claimed the small building was where the Finns "worshipped their gods, calling upon them to bring rain and good harvests to Finns, and wrath upon their neighbors." An investigation by other residents, however, revealed that the "motive was not godliness, but cleanliness."[78]

A chimneyless *kiuas* ("stove") built of fieldstone heats the *savusauna* at the Finn Creek Museum near New York Mills during the 1970s. On top of the stove is a metal container that provided heated water for bathing.

By the 1920s, the traditional kiuas began to be replaced with a metal stove heated by a firebox that had a compartment for the pieces of fieldstone; a stovepipe and chimney directed the smoke outside, and a dressing room was attached to the steam room. Saunas built of sawn lumber became commonplace on farms and at lakeshore cabin sites by the 1930s and 1940s; once electric and gas stoves were introduced during the 1950s, the sauna emerged as a fixture in numerous homes, health clubs, spas, resorts, and motels.

Religion, Politics, and Organizations

Minnesota's Finns formed numerous ethnic organizations, ranging from churches and temperance societies to

Three men in a sauna, which includes a chimney and dressing room, on Jacob Hoikka's farm located close to Annandale. One man pours water on the hot stones to create *löyly* ("steam"), 1960.

cooperatives and radical political groups. These organizations played a vital role by assisting the Finns in surviving the conditions they encountered in America and in maintaining their cultural heritage. The diversity of institutions, however, also reflected the often contentious nature of the Finnish immigrant experience in the New World setting.

Several Lutheran Paths to Heaven

While the vast majority of religious Finns were Lutherans, differences developed within the ranks of the estimated one in four who pursued a spiritual life in America. Many early émigrés had been influenced by the teachings of Lars Levi Laestadius, a pietistic and charismatic nineteenth-century religious revivalist from northern Sweden who inspired a considerable following among Finns in the Nordic Arctic region. One historian of Finnish American religious movements has observed that Laestadians (also called Apostolic Lutherans) didn't follow the directives of pastors and officials associated with the state church of Finland; instead, "they received their inspiration and direction from the elders of Lapland who warned the true believers to remain apart from 'the flock of the world and the heretics who condemn the [Laestadian] Christians.'" Indeed, the Laestadians were so closely tied to religious movements in northern Finland and Sweden "that in many respects it seemed as if the Atlantic Ocean did not exist." And, unlike standard Lutheran practices that typically admitted all baptized and confirmed individuals to church membership, only the "reborn" could join Laestadian congregations. Early Laestadians preferred to reside in rural areas, where believers could follow "a Spartan, family-centered life-style emphasizing faith and hard work."[79]

Cokato's Laestadians built Minnesota's first Finnish church in 1874; another six would appear in the state by

The Runeberg Apostolic Lutheran Church (Runeberg Township, Becker County), here in 2006, has changed very little since it was built in 1938; the church continues to serve a large congregation and Sunday school. Besides Runeberg, eight other Apostolic/Laestadian Lutheran churches that belong to four different federations still function in the small towns and rural areas of Minnesota's "Finnish Triangle": Wolf Lake (two) and Spruce Grove townships (Becker County); Newton Township and New York Mills (Otter Tail County); and Menahga (two) and Sebeka (Wadena County).

late 1888, including the diminutive Holmes City church, which still retains many of its original 1877 interior furnishings. Franklin's Laestadians organized a congregation in 1873 and built their rural church a few years later; the community experienced "a rigorous revival of Laestadian principles" when Angelica Jokela, a daughter of Laestadius, immigrated to Franklin in 1880. Four early churches were founded in the New York Mills area; one embraced Minnesota's largest congregation. By 1926, the state's forty-two Laestadian congregations included 7,720 members, 85 percent of them rural. The membership grew thereafter, but doctrinal differences divided the greater group into several federations.[80]

A second expression of religious life occurred when a number of autonomous congregations, professing "the evangelical Lutheran faith," emerged during the 1870s and 1880s. In 1886, a few representatives from these churches came together in Minneapolis to discuss the possibility of establishing an association of Finnish Lutheran congregations. This effort proved unsuccessful, but in 1890 the Finnish Evangelical Lutheran Church of America (Suomi Synod), modeled somewhat after Finland's state church, was formed in Hancock, Michigan. By 1926, Minnesota had forty Suomi Synod congregations (twenty-eight rural) with 5,820 members. One of the largest, Virginia's Finnish Evangelical Lutheran Church (named Zion in 1948), was created as an independent congregation in 1894; the church was built in 1896, accepted by the congregation in 1897, and dedicated in 1903; Suomi Synod affiliation occurred in 1918. The church sponsored several programs, including athletic teams and Finnish language, history, and culture classes for children that continued to 1948. An English-language Sunday school program was introduced in 1932, although the church minutes were written in Finnish until 1945. Its pastors also served congregations in Mountain Iron, Palo, Markham, Alango-Field, Idington, Cook, Orr, and Emo, Ontario. In

Virginia's Finnish Evangelical Lutheran Church (c. early 1900s) was renamed Zion in 1948 and Gethsemane following a merger in 1963; the building was razed in 2006.

1963, Zion merged with another congregation, organized in 1894 by Virginia's Swedes and Finland Swedes, to form Gethsemane Lutheran Church.[81]

Finnish Lutherans who disagreed with what they perceived as the synod's authoritarianism and overly powerful clergy formed a "People's Church" in 1898. Officially termed the Finnish-American National Evangelical Lutheran Church, thirty Minnesota congregations (twenty-six rural) counted 2,525 members in 1926. Since many congregations were small and widely dispersed, a clergyman reached them only one or two Sundays a month. One such pastor was the indefatigable Rev. E. W. Niemi, who trekked to nine far-flung flocks in five counties.[82]

Because of doctrinal divisions, even small Finnish settlements could include more than one Lutheran church. Furthermore, America's religious pluralism attracted some Finns to denominations other than Lutheran. From 1891 to the 1920s, Minnesota's Finns affiliated with six other Protestant groups and formed thirty congregations: twelve Congregational, ten Methodist, three Pentecostal, two Unitarian, two Baptist (including a short-lived Chisholm group, organized in 1953), and one Salvation Army. Half developed in the multicultural environment of the Iron Range, although Menahga Finns established Pentecostal, Methodist, and several Lutheran congregations.[83]

The earliest non-Lutheran group, a Methodist congregation, appeared seven miles west of Moose Lake in 1891. One year later a log chapel was dedicated on Midsummer's Day—the first Finnish Methodist church in North

America. The Revs. Matti and Elin Pitkanen (the latter ordained in 1928 as the nation's first female Methodist minister) served several congregations from 1928 to 1949. Finnish Congregational Church missionaries from Ohio and New England also began working in a few areas of Minnesota during the 1920s. The largest congregation and church emerged in Cloquet, but by 2012 the Finnish Congregationalist tradition continued in just two St. Louis County places, located eighteen miles apart: Palo and Bassett.[84]

Two notable people in the religious life of Minnesota's Finns were Risto and Milma Lappala, whose liberal theology led them from Congregationalism to Unitarianism. In 1911–12, the Lappalas established the world's first Finnish Unitarian congregation and church in Virginia, thereby providing an alternative to Lutheran and Socialist Finns who often were at odds on the Mesabi. (Alango Township's Unitarians organized in 1916.) After Risto Lappala died in 1923, his wife continued their ministry, "carrying the message of immigrant's rights, women's rights, social justice, reason, and peace" until her death in 1950. The Virginia congregation is still active today.[85]

Temperance and Fraternity

The first institutions that arose in most Finnish communities were church related—except on the Iron Range, where temperance societies often preceded religious organizations. The temperance movement developed when concerned Finns acted to curb the excessive drinking of young men attracted by the temptations of saloon life and inexpensive alcohol in America.[86]

Minnesota's initial Finnish temperance society and hall, *Pohjan Leimu* ("Northern Light"), appeared in Soudan in 1886. During subsequent years, more than twenty additional temperance groups developed on the Iron Range, often on land donated by mining companies. Overall, at least fifty Finnish temperance halls emerged throughout Minnesota, with most chapters later joining one of three national Finnish American associations.[87]

Since temperance received strong support from religious Finns, dances were banned from most halls. Opposition to these restrictions, as well as philosophical divisions, saw some halls transform into workers' and Socialist clubs where dancing, card playing, and Marxist discussions were permitted. The temperance movement experienced a rapid decline following passage of the nationwide prohibition amendment in 1919. By 1941, only sixteen Finnish chapters with 650 members remained in Minnesota; all had vanished by 1960.[88]

In 1898, the Knights and Ladies of Kaleva—an institution that sought to protect and perpetuate Finnish culture in North America—was organized in Montana. Minnesota's first Kaleva society, the Otava Lodge of Eveleth/Gilbert/Sparta, appeared in 1900, and eleven more lodges were organized from 1901 to 1927. The only secret order created by Finnish immigrants, the Knights and Ladies "aimed to enlighten the Finnish community, preserve its traditions, and cultivate the Finnish national spirit." Some Kaleva lodges developed lakeside camps where children learned Finnish and members could engage in sauna going, swimming, socializing, and celebrating their Finnishness. Kaleva Island (*Kalevasaari*) on Long Lake, started in 1924 by the Eveleth lodge, still remains active, as does Sampo Beach (*Samporanta*), developed on Little Grand Island Lake in 1939 by Duluth's Kaleva society.[89]

Right and Left in Political Life

Rural, nineteenth-century Finnish immigrants had little interest in partisan politics, but the financial panic of 1893 during Democratic President Grover Cleveland's administration led many to the Republican Party. Some descendants of these Finns, even during the 1970s, still referred to the "Cleveland hard times" experienced by their parents and grandparents.[90]

The first Minnesota Finn elected to political office beyond the local level was Charles Kauppi of Duluth, who, at age fifteen in 1879, immigrated to his family's Midway Township homestead. In 1896, Kauppi, now a Republican businessman, was elected to the first of five four-year terms as a St. Louis county commissioner. Meanwhile, on the Iron Range, Republican John Saari of Sparta served two terms (1905–8) in the Minnesota House of Representatives; since then, more than fifteen people of Finnish descent have followed Saari to the legislature.[91]

The only Finn elected to national political office was two-term (1921–25) Minnesota Republican Congressman Oscar J. (Väänänen) Larson. Born in Finland, raised in Michigan's Copper Country, and educated as an attorney, Larson moved to Duluth in 1907. A personal friend of presidents Theodore Roosevelt and Herbert Hoover, Larson was praised by supporters for "progressive Americanism" but roundly criticized by foes for opposing left-wing causes. Despite Larson's electoral success, "very little cooperation in politics [occurred] among right-wing Finnish-Americans." Instead, it was the Finnish American left that most strongly influenced Minnesota politics during the first decades of the twentieth century. As Reino Kero has noted, "American politics had three immigrant groups: 'old,' 'new' and the Finns."[92]

The reasons for the leftward political tilt of many Finnish Minnesotans are complex, but it is important to note that late-nineteenth- and early-twentieth-century immigrants were influenced by experiences and events—ranging from bread riots to labor unrest—caused by czarist oppression in Finland. Many opposed organized religion, choosing instead to develop workers' societies and halls and join America's growing Socialist movement. "Socialism provided them, not with the antithesis of faith and reason,"

Oscar J. (Väänänen) Larson (1871-1957) graduated from Northern Indiana Normal School (now Valparaiso University) in 1891 and the law department of the University of Michigan in 1894. He worked on numerous Finnish American causes after moving to Duluth in 1907, but the campaign materials for his successful 1922 congressional run, such as this newspaper advertisement, made no mention of Larson's ethnic background.

states sociologist Peter Kivisto, "but with a profound faith in reason." Also important was the leadership provided by the "Apostles of Socialism," a cadre of Finnish intellectuals who transmitted leftist political concepts to their immigrant colleagues. Finns boasted high literacy rates, and miners and timber workers who encountered exploitation and the perils of industrialization on a daily basis, along with farmers who resided on marginal agricultural holdings, read radical newspapers avidly. Overall, an estimated 25 to 40 percent of Finnish immigrants participated in some facet of left-wing political, social, and cultural life.[93]

The first Finnish American Socialist chapter emerged in

Finnish Halls

Finnish halls, typically sponsored either by temperance or workers' organizations, were extremely important features of immigrant community life. Temperance programs addressed the perils of excessive alcohol consumption, whereas left-wing halls promoted workers' political causes. Many participants, however, were drawn to the halls' lending libraries, socials, plays, movies, lectures, debates, concerts, and athletic events. Dances, popular in workers' halls, were typically banned from temperance halls associated with churches.

The *Valontuote* ("Product of Light") Temperance Society of Virginia, founded in 1893, opened this hall in 1906. When Valontuote was deactivated in 1966, the town's Knights and Ladies of Kaleva purchased the hall, shown here in 2005, which now serves as a community social and cultural center. It was listed in the National Register of Historic Places in 1979.

Play scripts, often borrowed from newspaper collections or Duluth playwright-director Lauri Lemberg, allowed immigrant laborers, farmers, housewives, and servants to transform themselves into thespians who performed before appreciative audiences. In 1915, Duluth's Finnish Workers' Opera presented an ambitious Finnish-language version of *Carmen* in the Orpheum Theatre.

Some temperance halls, as in Nashwauk and Zim, were later transformed into Socialist institutions when members with sympathies for workers' causes formed a majority. Temperance often remained part of the new agenda, but now dancing, card playing, and Marxist discussions were permitted. Eventually, divisions within the Finnish left could lead to separate workers' halls in the same community. In rural Sebeka-Menahga, two halls emerged in the 1920s: the West hall's membership was aligned with the cooperative movement, whereas the East's supporters—some of whom later departed for Soviet Karelia—were committed to radical causes. In Minneapolis, a small group of Communists used their "loud voice" to gain control of the Finnish Socialist hall during the 1930s, but when they failed to meet their mortgage obligations the building was vacated and later razed; following the takeover the Socialists transferred their meetings to the Wells Settlement House.[viii]

The Finnish Socialist Opera of Virginia, built in 1913, was renowned for its architectural features and programs and also served as the headquarters for two major strikes—by Mesabi miners (1916) and north woods timber workers (1917). The hall stands today, but its ornate proscenium arch, baroque-style auditorium, and pool (located under the stage floorboards to represent lakes, rivers, and oceans) were gutted and replaced by offices and meeting rooms in 1958.

Massachusetts in 1899, two Socialist newspapers appeared shortly thereafter, and a national organization, the Duluth-based Finnish-American Labor League, was formed in 1904. Delegates attending the league's 1906 meeting in Hibbing voted to join the American Socialist Party (ASP) and change the name to the Finnish Socialist Federation (FSF). The FSF was the first foreign-language group to unite with the ASP and served as its largest non-English-language chapter for several years. When the ASP's Finnish membership peaked at 13,665 in 1913, at least 30 percent were Minnesotans—the highest representation from any state.[94]

Finnish mine workers participated in several spontaneous Mesabi strikes from 1893 to 1905; three of them were shot and killed by marshals and deputies. A more disciplined approach to labor action occurred in 1903 when a significant number of Minnesota's Finnish Socialists affiliated with a group that was organizing workers on the Mesabi: the Western Federation of Miners (WFM). Four years later, in 1907, the WFM initiated a two-month-long strike that involved thousands of mine workers, a large majority of them Finns. When the strikers' demands for increased pay, improved working conditions, and union recognition proved unsuccessful, mining company officials blacklisted many Finns they identified as militants and "troublemakers." Soon, the "forced migration" of Finns to Minnesota timber camps and western mining districts was under way, although when a "Finnish troublemaker had money," more than likely "he established a farm"—often in the cutover region. In St. Louis County alone, the number of rural Finns increased from 1,300 to 3,535 between 1905 and 1910.[95]

Numerous Mesabi residents and organizations damned the strikers' actions, including conservative Finns who issued proclamations that "abhorred and condemned" the radicals' socialistic "East-Asian barbarism," most notably their "inflammatory speeches disgracing the Christian religion and civilization." Early-twentieth-century racial stereotyping, which contended that Finns were of Mongol origin, also compounded their image as drinkers, brawlers, and knife fighters. One famous court case of January 1908—a St. Paul district attorney's ruling that turned down the citizenship applications of John Svan and fifteen other FSF members because of claims Finns were not white—was an overt effort to establish "an explicit linkage between race and political radicalism." The decree was reversed a few weeks later when a Duluth district court judge ruled that even though Finns may have been "Mongols" in the past, subsequent intermixing with Teutonic peoples had made them "among the whitest people in Europe."[96]

Deep internal fissures also plagued the Finnish political left just a few years later. Radical Finns from Minnesota, the Midwest, and the West generally embraced the direct political action espoused by the Industrial Workers of the World (IWW), whereas East Coast Finns opted for traditional parliamentary socialism. Duluth was the headquarters for two important Finnish IWW institutions: *Industrialisti*, a Finnish-language newspaper, and the Work People's College (*Työväen Opisto*), which began in 1903 as a folk and theological training school for the Finnish National Lutheran Church before being taken over by industrial unionists four years later. The schism between social democrats and IWW advocates became so pronounced in 1914 that some three thousand members, the largest number from Minnesota, withdrew from the FSF; they maintained their IWW allegiance by forming the Finnish Industrial Union (FIU).[97]

When Mesabi miners engaged in a spontaneous strike during June 1916, FIU organizers met with other ethnic groups in Finnish workers' halls, where they convinced their colleagues to request IWW assistance. Although eight to ten thousand workers struck for two months, their efforts proved fruitless. Minnesota's reactionary governor, John Burnquist, who allowed U.S. Steel to employ a thousand-man private army that terrorized the strikers and killed

A 1931 notice for the Duluth Work People's College (*Työväen Opisto*), an institution supported by members of the Industrial Workers of the World, one of only two higher educational institutions developed by Finns in North America. The college functioned until 1941, when the building was converted into apartments; it still stands in Duluth's Smithville neighborhood.

This Is the School the Workers Built

IT WELCOMES YOU

The Following Courses Are Taught:

Marxian Economics	Organization Methods	Bookkeeping
Sociology	Labor Journalism	Mathematics
History of Labor	Public Speaking	Blue Print Reading
Movement	English	and Allied Subjects

THIS SCHOOL IS RUN BY WORKERS FOR WORKERS

IT IS OPEN FROM DECEMBER 1st TO MARCH 30th
It Costs You $39.00 per Month

SUMMER SCHOOL FOR JUNIORS:
June 22nd to July 17th for those aged 15 to 20
July 20th to August 14th for those from 12 to 15.

FOR FURTHER INFORMATION APPLY TO

WORK PEOPLE'S COLLEGE
Box 39, Morgan Park Sta.   Duluth, Minnesota

two of them, strongly influenced the outcome. In 1917, at Burnquist's urging, the Minnesota legislature created the Commission of Public Safety, which placed significant restrictions on individuals and organizations deemed anti-American. Soon, left-wing Finns were subjected to violent acts committed by both official and ad hoc groups: National Guard troops ransacked Mesabi workers' halls and Duluth's IWW office; a new Work People's College building was destroyed by a suspicious fire; IWW leaders were arrested; young Finnish men who failed to register for the military draft were harassed or indicted; and one Finn was lynched by Duluth vigilantes. Assisting the commission were O. J. Larson and other conservative Finns who formed the Finnish-American Loyalty League, which later merged with the national Lincoln Loyalty League. Despite the unfavorable political environment, north woods lumberjacks or "timberbeasts," many of them Finns, engaged in a 1917 strike that also proved unsuccessful.[98]

A Hanging and a Lynching in Duluth

Duluth's first legal hanging occurred in September 1885, several months after John Waisanen, a twenty-three-year-old Finnish miner, was charged with murdering a Tower Irish Canadian liquor distributor. The hanging occurred outside the St. Louis County courthouse, where it was witnessed by seventy-five sheriffs, policemen, clergymen, journalists, and interpreters, who exclaimed "there could not be better work done" and approved of the "ease with which the execution had been carried out." After the noose was removed from Waisanen's neck, a crowd of onlookers rushed the gallows and began "cutting pieces of the rope as souvenirs." His corpse was placed in a coffin and transported by horse cart to an unmarked grave in the poor farm cemetery.

Memories of the hanging lingered in northeastern Minnesota for a decade. When a Finn stabbed and wounded a Biwabik South Slav in 1894, the perpetrator was threatened with hanging. "Threats don't count," argued Tower's newspaper. "A piece of rope does better work. If necessary give it to them." In September 1918, Finnish laborer Olli Kiukkonen (often misspelled Kinkkonen) was tarred, feathered, and lynched by members of the Knights of Loyalty, a vigilante group that harassed immigrants who failed to register for the military draft. When Kiukkonen's body was discovered in October, Duluth's coroner absurdly claimed the thirty-eight-year-old Finn had been shamed into committing suicide after renouncing his intentions to become an American citizen. The *Duluth News Tribune* agreed, asserting that the "Judas" Kiukkonen, "who went out and hanged himself," deserved to die; "forget him," exhorted the newspaper. Probably because foreign-language newspapers were subjected to governmental censorship during wartime, the Finnish left-wing press did not agitate for an investigation. Instead, it was Irishman Jack Carney, editor of *Truth*, a local Scandinavian Socialist newspaper, who vigorously condemned the lynching. Kiukkonen certainly did not kill himself, insisted Carney, declaring that the victim's willingness to stand up for his rights and those of other workers made him "feared by the businessmen of this city, including his own countrymen." Despite Carney's protestations, the perpetrators were never arrested or identified.[ix]

OLLI KINKKONEN
1881 ——— 1918
VICTIM OF WARMONGERS

Following the discovery of Olli Kiukkonen's body in October 1918, about a month after his death by lynching, the Finnish laborer was buried in an unmarked grave in Duluth's Oneota Cemetery. The gravesite was identified and marked in 1978, but Kiukkonen's surname is still misspelled on his headstone.

The Russian Revolution, the emergence of a Communist government in the Soviet Union in 1918, and the formation of the Communist-backed Workers Party of America (WPA) in 1922 led to a second schism within the Finnish American left. The Finns' working-class movement was now divided into three major groups: Socialists, industrial unionists, and Communists. By 1923, Finns constituted 45 percent of the WPA's membership, with St. Louis and Otter Tail counties identified as the major centers of such activity. Midwestern and western Finns who didn't join the WPA typically remained as members of a much smaller IWW, while East Coast Finns retained their Socialist affiliations.[99]

In 1924, when the Communist International called for an end to all foreign-language federations, Finnish American locals were rendered quite powerless since authority now passed directly from the WPA's leadership to the Comintern in Moscow. Only about two thousand Finns chose to remain with the WPA, and additional members were purged and expelled from the party between 1928 and 1930 for "bourgeois leanings and adherence to social-democratic ideas." Nevertheless, some second-generation Finnish Americans would fill major positions in the WPA and its affiliated organizations. In 1930, when Rudolph Harju ran as the Communist Party candidate for Minnesota's U.S. Senate seat, he was serving as executive secretary of the United Farmers League—a radical organization formed in North Dakota in 1926 which moved its headquarters to New York Mills four years later. More visible was Gus Hall (Arvo Halberg) of Cherry Township; after being elected to the national executive board of the American Communist Party in 1946, Hall held several major leadership positions for more than forty years and served as the party's four-time U.S. presidential candidate.[100]

A further decline in radical numbers occurred from 1931 to 1934 when some eight thousand first- and second-generation Finns, perhaps a thousand from Minnesota, de-

parted North America for the Karelian Autonomous Soviet Socialist Re-
public (KASSR), where they hoped
to participate in establishing a workers' utopia. Many Minnesota Finns
who succumbed to "Karelian Fever"
(*Karjalankuume*) were from timber
camps and the Iron Range, although
an appreciable number resided in
rural places. The entire group of
KASSR-bound Finns included committed Communists as well as ideal-
ists; others simply hoped to improve
their perilous economic situation
during the Great Depression.[101]

Soon after arriving in the KASSR,
the Finns suffered considerable hard-
ship and deprivation when Soviet au-
thorities viewed them with suspicion
because of their American connections. An unknown number (perhaps 40 percent) eventually managed
to leave or escape the Soviet Union

Arthur Leskela emigrated from Finland in 1905 and
later served as a U.S. soldier during World War I.
Leskela worked as a miner throughout the United
States but maintained a residence in Otter Tail
County, where he was buried following his death in
a Lead, South Dakota, gold mine cave-in. Lutheran
and Methodist funerals were conducted for Leskela,
although his Marxist political sympathies are de-
picted by the headstone's hammer and sickle.

and return to Finland or North America, but most weren't as
fortunate. Tragically, thousands of Finnish men from North
America and Finland were assassinated during the Stalin-
ist purges of 1936–38, including Oscar Corgan, who had recruited Minnesotans to the KASSR a few years earlier. Corgan's daughter Mayme later recounted the horror of those
years: the Finns' "adopted country," she wrote, had quickly
turned into "a terrifying prison." From 1989 until her death
in 2004, the tireless Mayme Corgan Sevander documented
the painful history of American Finns in the KASSR, doing
much investigative work in Duluth, the sister city of Petroza-
vodsk, her home in Russian Karelia.[102]

Although their numbers didn't approach those who

left for the KASSR, from 1936 to 1938 at least one hundred Finnish Americans (one-fourth of whom died) volunteered to serve with the 2,800-man Abraham Lincoln Brigade that fought against Fascist forces during the Spanish Civil War. Overall, one in four of these Finnish Americans had some connection with Minnesota, the largest representation from any state; furthermore, they constituted 40 percent of the sixty Minnesotans who joined the brigade. No Minnesotan achieved the notoriety of New York Finnish American William Aalto, whose wartime feats are likely represented by Robert Jordan, the enigmatic hero in Ernest Hemingway's novel *For Whom the Bell Tolls*. Two of six Finnish Minnesotans killed in Spain received special recognition for their bravery, however: Commander Reino Tanttila of Zim, termed by a fellow volunteer as "the bravest comrade I ever knew" before dying of wounds in 1936, and the "unassuming" Lieutenant Henry Buska of Cromwell, who led his troops in capturing three hundred prisoners before he was captured, tortured, and executed in 1938.[103]

Surviving volunteers such as Martin D. Maki often experienced discrimination upon their return to the United States. Arriving in Minneapolis in 1939 after a year in a Spanish prisoner-of-war camp, Maki was fired from several jobs over the next three years for his brigade associations. Describing himself as a "serious person who intensely hated Fascism," Maki volunteered for the U.S. Army in 1942 and received two battle stars for bravery. Despite his distinguished record, he still faced employment difficulties, only realizing job security after joining the Minneapolis Carpenters Union in 1948. Upon his death in 2001 at age eighty-nine, Maki was eulogized as a lifelong "incredible idealist."[104]

Most Finnish leftists were avid supporters of Minnesota's Farmer-Labor Party during the 1930s. Since President Franklin Roosevelt's agenda embraced several progressive Farmer-Laborite causes, these Finns also became strong New Deal advocates. Nowhere was Finnish exuberance for Farmer-Labor causes more evident than at Mesaba Cooperative Park, which left-wing Finns developed in 1929 on a 160-acre property located eight miles east of Hibbing. Until the outbreak of World War II, thousands of people attended the park's annual summer "festivals of struggle," where political speeches, athletic competitions, plays, musical performances, and dances were featured. Among the park's strongest supporters were numerous second-generation Finns, some of whom assisted in organizing a successful timber workers strike in 1937 and in unionizing steel and mine workers during the late 1930s and early 1940s. Thus, after years of effort, politically progressive Finnish Minnesotans had finally moved "into the mainstream of American labor organization and political life with opportunities to influence their destinies far beyond their ethnic community."[105]

For STATE SENATOR
57TH DISTRICT

Mrs. Viena P.
JOHNSON
Endorsed by FARMER - LABOR Ass'n.

Vienna Pasanen Johnson (the daughter of Ida Pasanen—a prominent Finnish Socialist and IWW organizer from Two Harbors) waged an unsuccessful campaign as the 1934 Farmer-Labor candidate for a state senate seat on Duluth's wealthy east side. An accomplished musician and tireless advocate for progressive causes, Johnson held numerous Farmer-Labor Party leadership positions during the 1930s and 1940s and was involved in negotiations that resulted in the merger and creation of the Democratic-Farmer-Labor (DFL) Party in 1944. The stamps on both sides of the image read "Union Made."

Cooperatives and the Common Good

Despite their differences, Finns representing a full range of political views—left, right, independent, and indifferent—often found reconciliation and agreement in an institution based on the common good: the cooperative. While Finns engaged in forming various types of cooperatives—boardinghouses, creameries and cheese factories, grain mills and elevators, automobile service stations and fuel distributorships,

telephone and electric companies, insurance associations and burial societies—the retail store was their most important and ubiquitous enterprise. "The Finns have learned," stated one commentator in 1930, "that the co-operative store is equally as important to each and every member as, if not more important than, their homes and farms."[106]

Minnesota's first Finnish cooperative store appeared in Menahga in 1903. The Menahga Cooperative Sampo and several similar stores that appeared shortly thereafter were typically developed to avoid exploitation by local merchants who monopolized economic activities in small communities. The concept received further attention in 1906 when delegates attending the Hibbing meeting of the Finnish-American Socialist Federation identified cooperatives as one way of dealing with working-class economic problems. During the Mesabi strikes of 1907 and 1916, Finns organized cooperative buying clubs when merchants denied them credit and service; some buying clubs later evolved into full-fledged stores. By 1917, Finns had organized thirty-three cooperative stores, thirteen on the Iron Range.[107]

Finnish cooperators quickly saw the need for a federation that would knit the disparate local societies together.

"Why shouldn't we gather our purchases into one?" they asked. "We could buy sugar, salt fish, and canned fish in quantities of many carloads," as well as "soap, coffee, and other merchandise." In 1917, the Cooperative Central Exchange (CCE) was organized in Superior, Wisconsin. Over the next forty-six years, CCE supported its affiliated cooperatives as a centralized purchasing association and by training employees and performing educational work.[108]

Between 1903 and 1929, Minnesota's Finns organized seventy-five cooperative stores. Despite their accomplishments, Finnish cooperators throughout the Midwest encountered considerable internal dissension during the 1920s. One group of cooperative activists, including members of the Communist-based Workers Party of America, believed that a movement supported by workers and farmers could not be separated from the "deep economic and social contradictions produced by the present class society." The other group advocated political neutrality, arguing that cooperative success would be accomplished only by appealing to a broad base of participants interested in achieving economic and social goals.[109]

Finnish cooperators faced a serious dilemma in 1929

The manager and three employees of the Virginia Work People's Association Cooperative stand in front of the store; the side awning displays the Finnish word for cooperative store: *osuskauppa.* On the street is the association's early 1920s International delivery truck.

when national WPA leaders demanded access to the $1.5 million of annual sales generated by the CCE. When CCE delegates gathered for a contentious annual meeting in April 1930, the Communists' request was voted down 186 to 43, essentially ensuring that a large majority of cooperatives would follow a politically neutral course. (These Finns, nevertheless, viewed the envisioned cooperative commonwealth as a "third way"—an alternative to both capitalism and communism.) The dissenters withdrew from the CCE and eventually controlled forty small "Unity Alliance" stores in the Upper Midwest, one-half in Minnesota. By 1945, only a few alliance outlets remained in the state, whereas some seventy stores were affiliated with the CCE.[110]

The CCE's training courses prepared hundreds of Finns for positions as store managers, bookkeepers, and clerks. Einar Kuivinen, the son of Finnish immigrants, found this training invaluable following his election as the first state president of a reorganized Minnesota Farmers Union in 1941. Raised in rural New York Mills, a community known for promoting "cooperatives for mutual benefits," and identified as an "extremely cooperative-minded" person, Kuivinen was president of the state's most liberal farmers' organization from 1942 to 1944 and 1946 to 1949, a time when it expanded from a few hundred members to nine thousand.[111]

Supporting Finland During the 1930s and 1940s

For centuries, Finland had remained a distant and unknown place to most Americans. But then, following the convergence of three events during the mid- to late 1930s, Finland suddenly found itself receiving considerable favorable attention from the American government and public. These same events would also contribute to unprecedented unity within the greater Finnish American community.

First was Finland's diligence in repaying its loans to the

United States. Finland was one of fifteen European nations that, from 1918 to 1920, borrowed money for relief and reconstruction purposes; the Finns used their loan to relieve a severe food shortage. In 1934, during the worldwide economic depression, Finland was the only nation that met its loan commitments. When U.S. Secretary of State Cordell Hull commented on Finland's willingness to keep "faith with its financial obligations," more than three thousand articles applauding the Finns'"consistent steadfastness" appeared in American newspapers.[112]

Second was the three-hundredth anniversary of the New Sweden colony, celebrated in 1938. It was originally intended as a singular Swedish American event: Finnish Americans were scheduled to mark their anniversary in 1941. The U.S. Congress, however, voted to combine both celebrations in 1937, and President Franklin D. Roosevelt quickly submitted a formal invitation to Finland. Former congressman Oscar Larson headed the national American-Finnish Delaware Tercentenary Committee, which commissioned Finnish sculptor Wäinö Aaltonen to create a large commemorative monument, dedicated in Chester, Pennsylvania, on June 29, 1938; the site included two benches fashioned from Minnesota granite. Ceremonies celebrating the Delaware valley settlement also occurred in several of Minnesota's Finnish communities, including a Cokato program attended by Governor Elmer Benson and several thousand people.[113]

Third was the Soviet invasion of Finland, anticipated during summer 1939 and initiated in late November. Concerns over the fate of the civilian population saw Duluth's Finns organize a General Relief Committee for Finland on November 7, followed two weeks later by the formation of a Help Finland Committee in Minneapolis. Both groups immediately began raising funds and collecting clothing and medical supplies.[114]

One week after the Soviet assault commenced on November 30, former U.S. President Herbert Hoover agreed to head the New York City–based Finnish Relief Fund, Inc., which would assist the "noncombatant population and the refugees who are the sufferers from unprovoked aggression." Hoover traveled both to Minneapolis and Duluth; the ten thousand people who gathered in the Minneapolis Auditorium on December 29—the largest single display of American support for Finland—heard Hoover, Minnesota Governor Harold Stassen, and U.S. Senator Henrik Shipstead extol the Finns' valor, pluck, and heroism. Among the Twin Cities groups offering assistance were Swedish and Norwegian organizations and churches; the Minnesota Artists Association, whose members donated some artworks for sale at auction; participants in "Take a Hand for Finland" card tournaments who gave their winnings to relief efforts; and two St. Paul radio stations that devoted some Sunday morning programming to Finnish topics. Elsewhere, seventy Minnesota communities organized Finnish Relief Fund committees, many headed by non-Finns such as Dr. L. W. Boe, president of St. Olaf College in Northfield. By the time the "Winter War" ended in March 1940, thousands of Minnesotans had contributed $150,000 toward Finnish relief.[115]

Hostilities ended when the Finns sued for peace in March 1940, but only after a hugely outmanned Finnish army inflicted severe losses upon Soviet military forces. In July 1941, however, the Soviet Union attacked Finland again, thereby initiating the "Continuation War." Many Relief Fund committees maintained their activities, with Duluth serving as the headquarters. Shortly after the conflict concluded in late 1944, the Relief Fund was replaced by a new organization, Help Finland, Inc., which functioned until 1950. Minnesotans persisted with their contributions, including a non-Finnish Minneapolis woman who gave five dollars for "poor little Finland"; Tower's relief committee, which sent eight dollars with a note, "we are all trying to do our bit"; and a Finnish woman from Ely who offered

Third-grader Osmo Hautala's drawing expresses the students' joy "when the American packages arrived" at Finland's Vimeli elementary school in 1949. "For the children," reported the school principal, the day was "better...[than] Christmas Eve."

a hundred dollars but with explicit instructions that it be used "only for the purchase of coffee."[116]

The Postwar Era

Finland may have maintained its independence, but the nation still faced years of austerity in coping with the aftermath of war. While Help Finland served as the official source of American assistance, thousands of Minnesota and North America Finns also sent money and untold numbers of parcels to their impoverished "old country" relatives. Six white-tailed deer from the state were even airlifted to Finland in 1948—fourteen years after an initial seven Minnesota deer had arrived. (Some fifteen thousand whitetails populated southern Finland by 2005.)[117]

Meanwhile, as the United States emerged as the world's leading postwar economic power, Finnish Americans participated in the growing prosperity. The two decades following the war saw large numbers of jobs, many offering high wages and generous benefits Finnish unionists had helped secure, emerge in northeastern Minnesota's revived mining industry. A steady stream of Finnish Americans

Finndians

Native Americans and Värmland Finns residing along the Delaware valley during the 1600s shared a "familiarity with forests, shamanism, hunting, fishing, and slash-and-burn farming" and also cohabited or married. About 250 years later, Ojibwe elder Paul Buffalo noted the similar practices of his people and northern Minnesota's Finns—hunting, fishing, farming, and trading. We "learned lots" from the Finns, Buffalo recalled. Certain writers and observers, however, claimed that Finns and Indians shared certain "primitive" characteristics that were deemed negative; some residents of the Lake Superior region also used a pejorative term, *Finndians,* to identify the children resulting from Finnish-Ojibwe unions. In Minnesota, however, Finndian has more recently become an honored and respected form of identity, undoubtedly because of the achievements many individuals who share this joint ancestry have attained in various professions, occupations, and other pursuits.[1]

Finndian artist Carl Gawboy of northeastern Minnesota, the son of a Finnish mother and Ojibwe father, is a retired Duluth college art instructor known for his depictions of the history, cultures, and landscapes of the Lake Superior region.

departed northern Minnesota, Wisconsin, and Michigan for the Twin Cities, where they pursued higher education or found employment as factory, technical, or service workers or in the professions.

Despite the improved economic conditions, some Finnish Minnesotans with ties to left-wing groups were subjected to investigation and harassment by governmental agencies during the 1950s, especially after Wisconsin senator Joseph McCarthy launched his demagogic Communist-hunting investigations. Mesaba Co-op Park, where thousands had once gathered, was a focal point for FBI surveillance; by 1959, the park's membership had declined so significantly that members considered disbanding the organization. Despite the dire outlook, a subsequent reorganization allowed a small group of dedicated volunteers to maintain the

"Flying Finns"

Finnish Americans in Minnesota and elsewhere participated in or avidly followed athletic events. Initially, wrestling drew large audiences, especially when a Finn such as Wäinö Ketonen, who held various world middleweight championships from 1914 to 1926, was featured. Boxing was a lesser attraction, although Finnish American Waldemar "Kid" Hasti and other pugilists fought in Cokato's temperance hall. Cross-country ski races were commonplace, and ski jumpers from Finland drew large crowds. Temperance and Socialist groups also sponsored gymnastics teams that performed pyramid building and other feats requiring both physical prowess and group cooperation.

Track and field events became extremely popular after long-distance runner Hannes Kolehmainen, the first "Flying Finn," won a total of four gold medals for Finland at the 1912 and 1920 Olympics. Five-time Olympic gold medalist Ville Ritola followed him, but no Flying Finn received more fame and attention than Paavo Nurmi, who garnered nine Olympic gold medals from 1920 to 1928. In 1913, Kolehmainen entered a six-mile race in Duluth, facing three runners who ran two miles each; when Kolehmainen won easily, "great crowds of Finnish people" rushed the track to congratulate him. Nurmi won fifty-three of fifty-five American exhibitions in 1924, including a one-mile race in St. Paul, where Ritola also broke the five-thousand-yard world record.

The notoriety of these athletes saw Flying Finns teams emerge in some Minnesota communities by the 1930s. One, the Flying Finns of New York Mills, reportedly secured "extra drive" by consuming fish, buttermilk, and Finnish bread during the halftime breaks of their basketball games. A successful Flying Finns baseball team from the Wright-Tamarack area of Carlton and Aitkin counties played its games on a cow pasture, used bats whittled from wood, and repaired worn baseballs by covering them with leather from old lumberjack boots. During the 1960s, the town basketball team in nearby Cromwell was named the Flying Finns.

No Flying Finns achieved more acclaim than the Embarrass High School track and field teams of the early 1950s, coached by Niilo Ed Hendrickson. Practicing on country roads and fields, the Embarrass team quickly became the smallest school to qualify for state championship competitions, finishing third and fifth in 1952 and 1953 respectively. Three Embarrass athletes were state champions: Warner Wirta in cross-country (1951) and the one-mile (1952), Ray Nevala in the quarter-mile (1953), and Casey Salo in pole vault (1954). The team's tenure as a track power ended in 1954 when Hendrickson accepted a high school coaching position at Edina in suburban Minneapolis, where he had a legendary career.

Other Finnish Minnesotans who have achieved notable athletic recognition are goalie Willard Ikola of Eveleth, elected to the U.S. Hockey Hall of Fame in 1984, and Janet Karvonen, Minnesota's first girls' basketball star, who led New York Mills to three state high school championships (1977–79) and scored 3,129 career points—a record not broken until 1997.[xi]

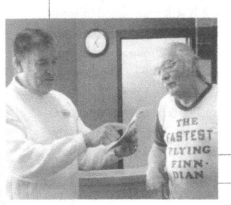

A member of the Flying Finns of Embarrass, Warner Wirta (right), the son of a Finnish father and Ojibwe mother, later competed with U.S. Army and Kansas State Teachers College teams and at the 1956 U.S. Olympics tryouts. Wirta later pursued a career as a teacher and as a social worker and advocate for military veterans. With Wirta in 2008 is Billy Mills, an Oglala Lakota who won a gold medal in the ten-thousand-meter race at the 1964 Olympics.

During the early 1950s, politically progressive Finns gathered in several of northeastern Minnesota's halls, such as in the St. Louis County township of Waasa, where they discussed the possible repercussions of the McCarran-Walter Immigration Act of 1952. Their concerns were fueled by the experiences of Finns such as Taisto Elo, a Minnesota lumberjack from Beaver Bay who spent time in prison during the early 1950s for his membership in the American Communist Party (1936–37) and was deported to Finland in 1953.

park as a recreational site for workers. Today, Mesaba Co-op Park is the most visible reminder of northeastern Minnesota's former Finnish radical movement, and it now supports an agenda that emphasizes progressive political action and programs promoting the causes of peace, labor, human rights, and environmental sustainability.[118]

Mainstream Finnish organizations also faced change and decline. Temperance activities, other than a few halls that now serve different purposes, are no longer evident in Minnesota, and only three Knights and Ladies of Kaleva groups remain active. Even the venerable cooperative movement that Finns supported so resolutely experienced a steady downturn, beginning in 1963 with the closing of the Superior wholesale facility and its merger with Midland Cooperatives, Inc., of Minneapolis. Because of rural depopulation, increasing retail competition, and the passing of the immigrant generation, most local cooperative stores were shuttered from the 1960s onward. The Cloquet store, once America's largest consumers' cooperative, shut down in 1977, including a major shopping center built twenty years earlier. The Finns' cooperative spirit is still manifested in some former stores that now serve as credit unions, convenience outlets, and gasoline stations; but only Finland and Wright have independent retail outlets that continue to follow the cooperative principles of their Finnish founders.[119]

Major changes also occurred within the Suomi Synod and Finnish National Church bodies. The synod joined the newly formed Lutheran Church of America (LCA) in 1963,

From the U.S. Civil War to the present, thousands of Finnish Minnesotans have been in the military, including nine sons (of fourteen children) of Finnish immigrants Jacob and Matilda Tompson (Pelkonen?), who served during World War II. The nine men (eight shown above in 1946) from rural Lawler represent one of the largest contingents of American brothers who served in the war; all returned home safely. In 1969, Army Specialist Fourth Class Dale Wayrynen, a fourth-generation Finnish Minnesotan from nearby Rice River Township (rural McGregor), received the Medal of Honor—the nation's highest military award—for sacrificing his life in 1967 to save several other soldiers. U.S. Highway 210 in Aitkin County now memorializes Wayrynen, as does the Dale Wayrynen Recreation Center at Fort Campbell, Kentucky.

while National congregations affiliated with the Lutheran Church–Missouri Synod one year later. Mergers occurring in communities with more than one Lutheran congregation often led to the sale or abandonment of churches. Further consolidations came after the LCA joined the Evangelical Lutheran Church of America (ELCA) in 1988.[120]

The Laestadians or Apostolic Lutherans, nevertheless, continue to maintain strong connections with Finland and their heritage, even as doctrinal differences or "schisms" have resulted in congregational alignments within several different federations. Some forty Apostolic/Laestadian churches remain throughout Minnesota, with the largest congregations found in the Twin Cities area, where at least six thousand members reside.[121]

Music, Literature, and Hollywood

Music, always an important feature in the lives of Minnesota's Finns, was initially performed in homes and churches. Familiar folk songs, often accompanied by an accordion or a violin or occasionally a *kantele* (Finland's national instrument), also became part of the musical repertoire. During the 1890s, community choirs and brass bands—typically sponsored by church, temperance, or workers' organizations and appealing to Finns and non-Finns alike—appeared in many communities, although dances in Finnish halls typically served as the most important social events. Songs describing the exploits and travails of working-class immigrants became extremely popular by the 1920s, especially those written or performed by three well-known IWW members who resided in northeastern Minnesota at various times: Arthur Kylländer, Hiski Salomaa, and T-Bone Slim (Matti Huhta).

The Third Generation, a Duluth-based family folk music group, attracted considerable attention from the late 1970s to the early 1990s for their interpretations of popular Finnish immigrant songs; one member, Gregg Santa, auditioned for and became a member of the Norwegian National Opera Company in 1997. Five Minnesota individuals and groups have been selected as Finlandia Foundation National Performers of the Year from 1996 to 2010: *Koivun Kaiku*, a kantele ensemble; singer-kantele player Diane Jarvi; pianist-conductor Craig R. Johnson; organist Vicki Gornick; and the dance band Finn Hall. Today, brothers Kip (Carl) and Eric Peltoniemi exemplify the Finnish American troubadour tradition with their performances and original songs, while the *Amerikan Poijat*, comprised primarily of Minnesota musicians, celebrates Finnish brass band history. Paul Metsa, from the Iron Range, has followed a different musical path, gaining recognition as a Twin Cities blues guitarist, vocalist, songwriter, and producer. *Kisarit*, a Twin Cities-based Finnish folk dance group, organized in 1972, has performed throughout North America and in Finland.

Classical music in Minnesota has been distinguished by two Finns: Tauno Hannikainen and Osmo Vänskä. Originally a cellist in Finland, Hannikainen studied with Pablo Casals before tran-

Four men with Finnish and Minnesota roots have been recognized as Fellows of the American Institute of Architects (FAIA), the organization's highest honor: Eino Jyring, Norman Perttula (practiced in Ohio), John Rauma, and David Salmela. One of the nation's iconic buildings, Christ Lutheran Church in Minneapolis, was designed by famed Finnish architect Eliel Saarinen and dedicated in 1949. An education wing, designed by Saarinen's equally famous son, Eero, was completed in 1962. The church received National Historic Landmark status in 2009 for its "adept use of materials, proportion, scale, and light."

The number of groups and events supported by Minnesota's Finns has declined over time, but the state still retains its position as a primary center for Finnish American activities. Many occur in the Twin Cities metropolitan area, where 42,910 people of Finnish descent resided in 2010—the largest concentration of urban Finns in America. Here, both scholars and the public draw upon the resources of

sitioning to orchestral conducting during the early 1920s. When directing the Duluth Symphony Orchestra from 1942 to 1947, Hannikainen received plaudits for his "authentic interpretations" of Sibelius; he subsequently directed major orchestras in Chicago and Helsinki. Decades later, Vänskä started his musical career in Finland as a clarinetist and eventually became a conductor and composer. Director of the Minnesota Orchestra since 2003, Vänskä has undertaken tours with his musicians that even included five performances (2005–9) in Cokato.

Some of the thirteen Finnish-language newspapers that appeared in Minnesota for varying periods of time from 1881 to 1980 (most in Duluth and New York Mills) also published novels, historical accounts, dictionaries, and American versions of the *Kalevala*.

For decades, the favorite musical performer among Finnish Americans was accordionist Viola Turpeinen (second from left, c. early 1950s), here in a humorous photograph outside of Cromwell. A native of Michigan's Upper Peninsula, the "accordion princess" made annual summer tours of Minnesota's Finnish dance halls from the mid-1920s until her death in 1958. Turpeinen's husband, William Syrjälä, a multi-talented musician from Cloquet, began accompanying Turpeinen in 1932 and continued as a solo performer from 1958 to 1992.

Lauri Lemberg's depiction of "living, loving, and fighting" in early-twentieth-century Duluth, serialized during the 1960s by a local newspaper, *Industrialisti,* was translated and published in 1992 as *St. Croix Avenue.* Shirley Waisanen Schoonover, a two-time O. Henry Short Story award recipient originally from Biwabik, wrote *Mountain in Winter,* a coming-of-age novel set in a northern Minnesota Finnish community; *Sampo: The Magic Mill* (1989), edited by Minnesotans Aili Jarvenpaa and Michael Karni, "offers an enriching view into the Finnish mind and soul." The journal *Finnish Americana* was published in the Twin Cities from 1978 to 1996 by Karni, while *The New World Finn,* a quarterly arts and literary tabloid, has been edited in Duluth since 1999 by Gerry Henkel. And Finnish Minnesotans Jim Johnson and Sheila Packa recently served two-year terms as Duluth's Poet Laureate.

American film and television includes two women with Finnish roots and Minnesota connections: Maila Nurmi and Jessica Lange. Nurmi attended Duluth schools during the 1940s and later moved to Los Angeles, where she became infamous as the campy Vampira, hosting television horror programs and starring in the outrageous film *Planet 9 from Outer Space.* Lange, from Cloquet, made her movie debut in 1976 and has subsequently received two Academy Awards (1982 and 1994).[xii]

the University of Minnesota, which offers some of the nation's best-known Finnish programs: language instruction, a preeminent Finnish American archival collection at the Immigration History Research Center, a visiting professorship in Finnish studies, and a fund for the performance of Finnish music.

Several Finnish-oriented organizations, events, and

activities that have developed since the 1950s trace their origins to Minnesota, such as St. Urho's Day, created in 1956 by Richard Mattson of Virginia. The fantastic legends associated with St. Urho, a fictitious patron saint who can be compared to Ireland's St. Patrick, have evolved over time. Today, the most common version, developed by Sulo Havumaki of Bemidji, describes the exploits of St. Urho, who saved Finland's grape crop thousands of years ago by driving out a huge infestation of grasshoppers. St. Urho celebrations typically occur on March 16, just before St. Patrick's Day, and often include purple wine and beer, humorous parades, and dances.[122]

Another event with Minnesota roots is FinnFest USA, which originated in the Twin Cities in 1983 and is now staged annually in alternating North American cities. Initially modeled after Finnish summer festivals once celebrated in North American communities, FinnFest now presents "Finnish and Finnish-American culture and heritage" and "brings modern Finland together with historic and contemporary America." Subsequent FinnFests have occurred

For centuries, Shrove Tuesday, the day before the beginning of Lent, has been celebrated as a wintertime sledding and sliding event (*Laskiainen*) in Finland. Since 1937, the rural St. Louis County community of Palo has sponsored an annual Laskiainen that occurs along Loon Lake over a February weekend. Here, a traditional Finnish *vipukelkka* ("whip sled") is used to propel a participant around a central pivot in 2011.

in Duluth (1992 and 2008) and again in Minneapolis (2002). FinnFest 2008 was highlighted by the presence of Finnish President Tarja Halonen, who received an honorary PhD from the University of Minnesota–Duluth. FinnFest is currently the largest Finnish event in North America, often attracting thousands of attendees.[123]

The most visible addition to the contemporary Finnish-Minnesota landscape is located outside of Bemidji, where Salolampi Finnish Village, one of fifteen Concordia Language programs, is located. The initial Finnish language program for children was offered at a rented site in August 1978. Nine years later, Concordia College, Moorhead, designated a forty-acre property along Turtle River Lake for the development of Salolampi Village, dedicated in 1988. A log sauna, donated from Finland, was erected in 1989, and nationwide fund-raising efforts conducted by the Salolampi Foundation, along with significant private gifts, culminated in 1993–94 with the dedication of three cabins from Finland and the construction of a main building, Jyringin Talo. (Salolampi now has eleven structures.) One- and two-week

Finnish President Urho Kekkonen (front left) met a large group of Finnish immigrants and their descendants in Esko on October 24, 1961, eight days after conferring with U.S. President John F. Kennedy during an official White House visit. Kekkonen's two-day, northeastern Minnesota stay also included a tour of the Iron Range, brief stops in Cloquet and Floodwood, and a speech at the University of Minnesota–Duluth.

Beatrice Luoma Ojakangas of Duluth, shown here with her collection of cookbooks, is a prolific author. *The Finnish Cookbook*, originally published in 1964, is now in its thirty-fifth printing, and her more than twenty-seven other books about food preparation have sold thousands of copies. Ojakangas is noted for her knowledge of breads and baking, which play a central role in Finnish cuisine. *The Finnish Cookbook* includes recipes for *ruisleipä* ("sour rye bread"), *pulla* ("cardamom coffee bread"), *Karjalan paisti* ("Karelian three-meat stew"), *pannukakku* ("oven pancake"), and *Karelian piirakka* ("rye-crusted rice-filled pie").

In the Twin Cities, Finnish immigrant Soile Anderson, who formed Deco Catering in 1981, has become widely known for her Finnish and Scandinavian foods; in 2003, she also established the Finnish Bistro, a St. Paul restaurant.

and a four-week high school credit course, as well as family and adult programs, are also offered at Salolampi.[124]

A majority of the almost one hundred thousand current Minnesotans who possess some Finnish ancestry do not engage in activities and events organized around their ethnic heritage. And only a small number of those who do participate are interested in learning about the contributions of Finnish Americans in shaping Minnesota's history. Such disengagement, of course, is true of many groups that, through the passage of time, have distanced themselves from their ethnic past.

Today, more Americans undoubtedly have greater awareness of Finland than they do of Finnish America. Their knowledge of Finland, however, is not limited only to the sauna and Sibelius. Contemporary Finnish design, architecture, music, and technology are frequently featured in American media; and Finland's high worldwide rankings in educational achievement, women's rights, environmental protection, trust in government, and quality-of-life indicators receive considerable notice. Ironically, knowledge of modern-day Finland may actually lead more people to the story of Finnish Americans—and to a renewed appreciation of their contributions to the fabric of Minnesota life.[125]

Finland Swedes

Finland Swedes (*Finlandssvenskar*) share a language with Sweden, but their history has been firmly rooted in Finland for centuries. Finland Swedes, often called Swede-Finns in North America, are concentrated along Finland's western and southern coasts and on the Åland Islands, which stretch southwestward toward Sweden. At the time of migration to North America, 13 percent of Finland's population spoke Swedish as their primary language; by 2011, only six percent did.[126]

Some estimates contend that Finland Swedes constituted up to 20 percent of Minnesota's entire Finland-born population, but these figures are much too high—especially for the twentieth century. In fact, it is not possible to determine with any certainty how many Finland Swedes resided in the United States prior to 1910, the year census enumerators began asking foreign-born respondents to provide their native language. But gaining an accurate count of Finland Swedes (or any language group) from 1910 onward still requires a laborious review of the manuscript schedules, although a recent computer program, using a one percent sample, can estimate their overall numbers. This program reveals that about seven percent of Minnesota's entire Finland-born population spoke Swedish in 1920, but the geographic accuracy of the results is inadequate. To circumvent this problem, much of the following discussion is based on a close review of the language listing for all of Minnesota's 29,100 Finland-born immigrants listed in the 1920 manuscript census. This assessment revealed that 1,705 Finland Swedes—six percent of all immigrants from Finland—resided in Minnesota. A few Finland Swedes settled throughout most of Minnesota, but the vast majority were concentrated in Duluth, the Twin Cities, and the Palisade area; on the Iron Range; and along the North Shore of Lake Superior.[127]

Twin Cities

Some writers have claimed that Minnesota's first Finland Swede came to Minneapolis in 1869; the 1860 census, however, lists Theodore Hubert, very likely a Finland Swede. The best-known early Finland Swede was Kustaa (Gustaf) Fredrick Bergstadius, who arrived in Minneapolis during the late 1870s as a ticket and immigration agent for the Chicago, Milwaukee, and St. Paul Railroad Company.

Bergstadius also assisted in founding two of South Dakota's Finnish settlements: Frederick (named for him) and Savo Township. Unlike other Finland Swedes, Bergstadius was a native of eastern Finland who spoke both Swedish and Finnish, and he eventually learned English. (Because Swedish is an Indo-European language, Finland Swedes had an easier time learning English than did Finnish speakers.) Bergstadius later used these linguistic skills when operating an immigrant employment agency and currency exchange in Minneapolis and while working for another Finland Swede, pharmacist Carl Södergren. Since Södergren's mail order department sold familiar and "authentic Finnish medicines," the pharmacy was well known both to Swedish- and Finnish-speaking immigrants residing beyond Minneapolis. Among the most popular products was a "balsam," advertised as the "best medicine for coughs, colds, and all illnesses of the chest and lungs."[128]

By 1920, Minneapolis was home to sixty-five Finland Swedes and St. Paul to forty-eight—respectively six and 50 percent of all Finland-born immigrants in each city. Included among the sixty-four adult men in both cities were twenty-one laborers, nine metalworkers, eight professionals and supervisors, seven carpenters, seven proprietors and salesmen, seven engaged in other skilled trades, and five pursuing miscellaneous occupations. Just nine women were employed: seven servants, one masseuse, and one seamstress. Twice as many Twin Cities Finland Swedes were married to a Swede or a Swedish American than to someone from their own ethnic group.[129]

Hopkins, west of Minneapolis, included twenty-five Finland Swedes—most residing on small truck farms. Some of the men began working at the Minneapolis Moline Power Implement Company's factory in Hopkins during the 1930s.[130]

Duluth

Northeastern Minnesota was the Finland Swedes' primary domain, and Duluth was their midwestern *Helsingfors*. Duluth's first pioneers settled by sawmills along the St. Louis River, including in their number Matt and Hannah Kynell, who arrived in 1882 from the lumber town of White Cloud, Michigan. Anticipating that Duluth would be a large city with urban comforts, Hannah Kynell was moved to tears when she instead saw wooden walkways and a crude waterfront.[131]

Only a few Finland Swedes resided in or maintained businesses and offices in downtown Duluth; one was attorney Charles Sawyer from the Åland Islands. A significant movement of Finland Swedes to West Duluth's large Swedetown started during the early 1900s. Here, many men, Matt Kynell among them, became known as carpenters and building contractors, notably the three Jacobson brothers (Jacob, John, and Joseph), who formed a construction company that built many major structures throughout northeastern Minnesota. Finland Swedes, by 1904, were operating a pharmacy, two saloons, and a grocery store that, in 1907, became the large West Duluth Mercantile Company on Ramsey Street; nearby was the West Duluth Realty Company, also owned by Finland Swedes.[132]

By 1920, the number of Finland Swedes in Duluth reached 542, or 14 percent of the entire Finland-born population. Some still resided along Garfield Avenue, close to the St. Louis River's shipyards and sawmills, but the largest concentration remained in West Duluth, where they clustered along Wadena and Ramsey streets and an area between Forty-eighth and Fifty-third avenues west. (A number of these homes were later razed for freeway construction.) The 253 employed males included 140 laborers; eighty engaged in skilled trades; twenty-three as proprietors, salesmen, supervisors, and professionals; and ten pursuing other occupations.[133]

Only twenty-six women, most of them unmarried, worked outside their homes in 1920: twelve laundresses, servants, and maids; six factory workers; five seamstresses and weavers; and three in professional and supervisory positions (a nurse, bank stenographer, and match factory inspector). Although Finland Swedes were less likely to have boarders than their Finnish-speaking compatriots, Hannah Kynell operated a boardinghouse on Nicollet Street for several years. In 1900, her house had nine boarders as well as the family's four children. After Matt Kynell's 1909 death, his fifty-six-year-old widow continued to operate the boardinghouse, which accommodated eight boarders and three of her adult children in 1910. By 1920, Hannah Kynell was living in her son's home, along with a Norwegian daughter-in-law, four grandchildren, and two boarders.[134]

Iron Range

When mining began in northeastern Minnesota, some Finland Swedes immediately made their way to the district; one, Gust Nyman, began working on the railroad between Two Harbors and the Vermilion Range in 1883–94 and was subsequently employed for almost forty years by the Oliver Iron Mining Company. Lutheran clergyman Carl Silfversten observed, nonetheless, that Finland Swedes were not keen on pursuing a "life in the mines." In fact, by 1920, only 442 immigrant Finland Swedes resided throughout the Iron

Politics

Finland Swedes did not engage in Minnesota's radical political movements as avidly as their Finnish-speaking cohorts. Nonetheless, some did participate in Iron Range labor events, including John Oman, the subject of a federal arrest warrant (later dropped) for serving as a strike leader at Ely's Chandler mine in 1904. Second-generation Karl Emil Nygard (1906–84), elected as the first Communist mayor of an American city (Crosby) in 1932, was Minnesota's best-known Finland Swede radical. The son of "a good strong Republican" father, Nygard (known as "Emil C." while mayor) was born in Iron Belt, Wisconsin, and raised in Crosby; thereafter his radicalism grew while attending the University of Minnesota for one year, followed by work experiences in Chisholm, Michigan, and Illinois. Returning to Crosby in 1929, Nygard worked as a miner and union organizer and ran unsuccessfully for mayor in 1930 and 1931. When Cuyuna Range economic conditions worsened and political unrest increased, the twenty-six-year-old Nygard, now running as the Communist Party candidate, was able to win a three-way race for mayor in 1932. Nygard's one-year term was stormy, and he was roundly defeated in 1933. He married in 1936 and moved to rural Becker County, eventually withdrawing from active politics because of the travel demands posed by his work as a dairy herd inspector.

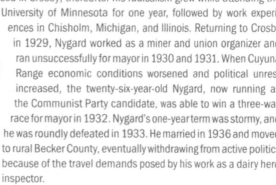

Karl Emil Nygard during the 1930s

Another second-generation Finland Swede followed a more conventional political path: C. Elmer Anderson (1912–98), who served both as lieutenant governor and governor of Minnesota. Anderson's Swedish-speaking parents emigrated from Finland during the late 1890s and settled in Brainerd, where Anderson began his career in local politics at an early age; in 1938, the twenty-six-year-old was elected lieutenant governor, serving on the ticket with Minnesota's "Boy Governor," Harold Stassen. Anderson held the position for a record eleven years and became governor in 1951 when Luther Youngdahl accepted a federal judgeship. Anderson defeated Orville Freeman in the 1952 election but lost to him two years later. Anderson then returned to Crow Wing County and reentered political life, serving as mayor first of Nisswa and later of Brainerd. Anderson's political pursuits ended in 1986 after he lost a four-way race for mayor in Brainerd. Minnesota's only governor with Finnish roots died in Brainerd at age eighty-five.[xiii]

Governor C. Elmer Anderson

Finland Swedes Herman and Johanna Shjal, who immigrated to Mille Lacs County's Bogus Brook Township during the early 1890s, moved to a ten-acre truck farm in northeastern Duluth in 1913. The Shjals transported their hand-washed vegetables to a Duluth market in a 1913 Model T Ford, which was also used to pull a plow and cultivator. Despite the farm's demanding physical work, the Shjals still refused public assistance when each was seventy-six in 1941, the year the photo was taken.

Range—less than five percent of the entire Finland-born population. The largest numbers lived in Eveleth (97), Hibbing (93), Chisholm (74), Virginia (49), and Crosby (41). Two-thirds of the employed males (155 of 248) were engaged in some facet of mining: eighty-three in mine-related construction and transportation, fifty-four as miners, and seventeen as supervisors and engineers. (Edward Smith, a Finland Swede, was St. Louis County's mine inspector from 1917 to 1941.) The ninety-four men who engaged in non-mining employment included forty laborers; twenty-four carpenters; sixteen working in other skilled trades; eight merchants, supervisors, and professionals; and six transportation workers. Later, after many of Eveleth's Finland Swedes moved out of mining into house construction, they reportedly formed "a monopoly on building work in the city." Just thirteen Iron Range females were employed as servants or cooks in 1920.[135]

Lake Superior's North Shore

Finland Swedes outnumbered Finns in most of the diminutive North Shore settlements that extended from French River toward the Canadian border. By 1920, the French River area (Duluth Township) was populated by twenty-seven Finland Swedes, while another seven resided a few miles to the northeast in Knife River. Farther northeast was the Lake County enclave of Larsmont, the only North Shore settlement where the immigrant Finland Swedes (18, with 50 American-born children) outnumbered Norwegians (12) and Swedes (8). Shortly after arriving in 1909, the Finland

Architect Anton Werner Lignell

Undoubtedly the first Finland-born professional architect to practice in Minnesota was Anton Werner Lignell (1867–1954), who emigrated from the Åland Islands to Butte, Montana, in 1888. Arriving in Duluth in 1903, Lignell established a brief architectural partnership with Frederick German, a collaboration that resulted in designs for several of Duluth's revival-style buildings, including the Glen Avon Church and large residences in the eastern mansion district. Lignell also designed two Minnesota courthouses, both now listed in the National Register of Historic Places: Cook County (with Clyde Kelly) in 1911–12, and the original (now privately owned) Roseau County courthouse (with Robert Loebeck) in 1913–14. Lignell designed the Duluth Steam Bath Company building in 1921 and continued to practice until the late 1930s; he later moved to Hawaii, dying there at the age of eighty-seven.[xiv]

This 1910 eclectic mission-style house, shown here in 2011, was designed by Anton Werner Lignell for Swedish immigrant and mining technology entrepreneur Gust Carlson and his wife, Hannah. It is one of the finest homes in the mansion district of East Duluth.

Swedes petitioned to have their settlement named Larsmo—the home community in Finland for several of them; however, when Duluth and Iron Range Railroad officials insisted on Larsmont, the residents "had to take it the railroad way." Another forty-four Finland Swedes were situated between Two Harbors and Larsmont, Two Harbors itself was home to thirty-seven, and twenty-five resided farther northeast in Silver Creek Township. Overall, 158 Finland Swedes lived between French River and Silver Creek in 1920.[136]

Almost all Finland Swede males in Two Harbors were railroad or dock workers. The small settlements and rural areas where most North Shore Finland Swedes resided, however, included lumberjacks who worked for the Alger-Smith Lumber Company and smaller logging firms and others who pursued fishing, farming, and a few public and private service jobs. At one time as many as fifty North Shore Finland Swedes, including several families, spent their summers on Tobin Harbor fishing camps, located at

Finland Swedes Charles Hill and son Reuben of Larsmont were among the North Shore's premier boat builders. Here, during the 1940s, Reuben works on the keel of the *Bluebird;* he died in 1997, at age ninety-two.

the northeastern end of Lake Superior's Isle Royale. Art Mattson, a second-generation Finland Swede, was the only commercial fisherman who retained his camp after Isle Royale National Park was established in 1940; until his death in 1982, Mattson fished and assisted Tobin Harbor's "summer people." Although not a commercial fisherman, his son Louis still holds a special-use permit to the Mattson camp.[137]

An additional thirty-one Finland Swedes (and twelve Finns) also lived in Minnesota's northeastern-most county, Cook. Most of these Finland Swedes resided inland from the North Shore, between Grand Marais and Hovland, where they engaged in subsistence homesteading and also worked as part-time loggers and fishermen. The twenty Finland Swedes in the Colville area, as well as the six residing close to Hovland, "cooperated both out of necessity and friendship" with their Norwegian and Swedish neighbors in developing community institutions and maintaining roads and bridges.[138]

Among the first Colville homesteaders were John (Jacobson) Jackson and his wife, Maria, who departed Eveleth in 1906, shortly after he survived several hours in a flooded mine—an accident that led to months of hospitalization and lifelong health problems. The family's situation grew so dire by 1920 that Maria Jackson and the family's two children returned to Finland, with expectations that John would later join them; however, when Maria realized that "life in Finland was even harder" than in Minnesota, she and the children returned within a year. Despite the extreme difficulties they encountered—six of eleven children did not survive to adulthood, a daughter was severely injured by a stray gunshot, their first house burned to the ground during the middle of winter, and two grandsons later drowned in Lake Superior—several members of the Jackson family, as well as a few neighbors, lived out their lives in far northeastern Minnesota. Survival, one daughter later wrote, was accomplished only by "hanging on."[139]

Rural and Agricultural Settlements

Finland Swedes were scattered throughout several areas of rural Minnesota, but even when they clustered together their numbers were seldom sufficiently large to give them an identifiable presence, most notably when nearby Finnish or Swedish immigrant communities were larger. This situation characterized the small settlements formed by farmers and laborers in three townships west and north of Duluth—Herman (16 Finland Swedes in 1920), Solway (21), and Rice Lake (17)—and farther north at Markham (20) and Makinen (16). Only one St. Louis County rural enclave— settled in 1907 and located six miles east of Cook along the East Little Fork River—was exclusively inhabited by Finland Swedes (16 in 1920). Much father to the south and located just outside the cutover region in Mille Lacs County was another group of Finland Swedes (25)—two-thirds of them concentrated in Bogus Brook Township, including six families who had originally settled in Hopkins.[140]

Minnesota's largest settlement of rural Finland Swedes emerged in Aitkin County during the 1890s when some immigrants moved from Duluth-Superior to the Mississippi River townships of Workman and Logan, served by the village of Palisade after 1909. Among the earliest were eight members of one family: Matt and Josephine Kullhem and their six sons, all born in Finland. Workman was unique in that its 1920 population of sixty-four Finland Swedes far exceeded the fifteen Swedes and one Finn

Olga Bergström, a Finland Swede, immigrated to Minnesota in 1903 and learned Finnish as a Hibbing boardinghouse servant. She married Finnish-speaking immigrant Edwin Petrell (Peltari) in 1905, and the couple established a small farm in northeastern Fairbanks Township, where she served as postmistress, learned photography, and hunted for small game. The family lived in Minneapolis, Chicago, and Seattle (1910–12 and 1917–31) before returning to the farm, where they resided until her death in 1941.

who lived there. Workman's Finland Swedes were seamlessly linked to the twenty-eight who resided in adjacent Logan Township. Another smaller settlement of Finland Swedes, located twenty miles southeast of Palisade and just north of Lawler, also dates to the late 1890s. The seventeen immigrant Finland Swedes who resided there in 1920 were situated on both sides of the Salo-Spalding township line, close to Sheriff Lake.[141]

Organizational Life

Some Finland Swedes sought to link their early organizations to those sponsored by Finnish-speaking immigrants. A few employed Finnish names, others were intended to serve as bilingual societies, and a small number attempted to affiliate with larger Finnish organizations such as temperance associations and the Suomi Synod. Language differences posed too great an obstacle, however, and the collaborations ended quickly. Thereafter, the institutional activities of America's and Minnesota's Finland Swedes focused on three major areas: religion, temperance, and benefit societies. From the 1930s onward, Finland Swedes also participated in the cooperative movement.[142]

One of the Finland Swedes' flagship institutions was organized in 1898 in West Duluth: the Swedish-Finnish Lutheran Evangelical Church. When it proved difficult to secure a permanent pastor in 1902, the congregation asked

The Finland Swedes' Bethel Lutheran Church of West Duluth, shortly after it was completed in 1916. Although the congregation disbanded in 1989 and the building was retrofitted for offices, its exterior appearance has changed very little up to the present.

members of Duluth's downtown Finnish church if they might be interested in sharing a bilingual clergyman. They received their answer later that year: "the Finns do not want to take part in the work with us." Ironically, two years after the Finland Swedes joined the Swedish Augustana Synod in 1907, their "Finnish brethren" inquired about the possibility of hiring a clergyman to serve both churches. But now it was the Finland Swedes' turn to say no, this time because "the two congregations belong to different synods."[143]

In 1912, the membership voted "to satisfy a wish among the young people" by changing the name to "Evangelical Lutheran Bethel Church"; four years later, the members dedicated their new church on Ramsey Street. Internal conflicts—termed a "spirit of unsettledness" by the Rev. Silfversten—affected the congregation in 1919, but the membership still expanded to several hundred people during the 1920s. Bethel also assisted in the formation of a small congregation of Swedes and Finland Swedes at French River in 1924 and sponsored the construction of its church ten years later. Despite these successes, the Rev. Silfversten still mourned the congregational divisions exhibited by his flock: if only "a better understanding and harmony [existed] between the people," he lamented, "we would have had one of the largest Lutheran churches in Duluth." On Easter Sunday 1989, after playing a major role in the religious life of West Duluth for almost seventy-five years, Bethel closed without fanfare or sentiment. "The congregation simply folded," recalled one observer, "and the pastor turned over the keys to the bishop of the local synod."[144]

Finland Swedes also organized about twenty Baptist congregations in the United States, including three in northeastern Minnesota. Immigrants who came from Finland's small group of Baptist churches started holding services in Duluth as early as 1893, and a "Mission Society" emerged in West Duluth by 1901, followed four years later by the organization of a congregation, Ebenezer Baptist. In 1908, plans were made for a building that would house stores on the first floor and a church on the second; a shortage of funds ended this plan, but the congregation succeeded in building a new church on a different West Duluth property in 1916. During the 1930s, some members of the Ebenezer congregation assisted with religious services conducted in the Larsmont school along the North Shore. The Ebenezer church served Finland Swedes until the early 1970s, when the congregation was disbanded and the building sold.[145]

In 1909, the Finland Swedes of East Little Fork River organized a small Baptist congregation; their church, also used as a community center, was built five years later. The building was razed after the congregation merged with the First Baptist Church of Cook in 1962. More long lived was the *Bethphage Svensk Finska Baptist Forsamling* of Chisholm, founded in 1906; the church was dedicated eight years later. When the Finland Swedes' Mission Union (a national organization formed in 1901) was disbanded in 1961, the congregation affiliated with the Baptist General Conference and became the First Baptist Church of Chisholm.[146]

Elsewhere on the Iron Range, Virginia's Swedes and Finland Swedes organized the Swedish Evangelical Lutheran

Mamre congregation in 1889. Similar collaborations occurred at Eveleth in 1897 (Swedish Evangelical Lutheran
Tabor), Hibbing in 1900 (Swedish Immanuel Lutheran),
Ely in 1902 (Swedish Lutheran Bethany), and Chisholm in
1906 (Salem Evangelical Swedish Lutheran).[147]

Finland Swedes and Swedes played an equal role in
building Palisade's Bethel Lutheran Church in 1924, but most
Sheriff Lake families chose a different religious path when
they formed a Scandinavian Assemblies of God congregation and later joined the Christian and Missionary Alliance.
Eventually the congregation constructed a tabernacle built
of materials salvaged from a vacant school. Not all Sheriff
Lake Finland Swedes chose to join the Pentecostal movement: one, Oscar Sundberg—fluent in Swedish, Finnish, and
English—headed the nearby Finnish Evangelical Lutheran
congregation of Tamarack when it was organized in 1915.[148]

The Finland Swedes' temperance movement emerged
in Massachusetts and Michigan during the late 1890s, and
a nationwide association was in place by 1902. Eveleth's
Runeberg temperance society, organized in 1898, was the
only Minnesota lodge in the early national association, but
others arose in Chisholm, Crosby, Hibbing, Palisade, Two

Members of West
Duluth's Finland
Swede temperance
society *Ljusstrålen*
("Beam of Light")
gathered, prob-
ably to celebrate
Midsommardagen
("Midsummer's
Day"), sometime
between 1904 and
1908.

Palisade's Mississippi Valley Rose (*Mississippidalens Ros*) Temperance Society had its own orchestral ensemble sometime between 1904 and 1917.

Harbors, and West Duluth by 1913. The Rev. Silfversten recalled how pleasing it was to see both West Duluth saloons operated by Finland Swedes go out of business soon after the local temperance group organized. Some lodges built halls where presentations and confessionals condemning the evils of drink were offered, although it was the social gatherings, musical programs, and athletic events that proved most popular. When the hall affiliated with Palisade's *Mississippidalens Ros* ("Mississippi Valley Rose") temperance organization burned in 1922, it was replaced by a new "Liberty Hall" that no longer maintained its temperance affiliation. Sited at a picturesque point along the Mississippi River several miles from a bridge crossing at Palisade, Liberty Hall quickly became a popular dance venue. Since Finland Swedes were located along both banks of the river, those who lived on the "other side" were ferried to and from the hall by boat; when the boatman was on the opposite bank, people would call out to him or ring a large cowbell hung from a tree. After the temperance group disbanded, the Palisade settlement maintained "little contact" with other Finland Swedes.[149]

Finland Swedes created their first mutual aid or sick benefit society in 1900 at Bessemer, Michigan, and similar groups quickly followed in Chisholm, Duluth, Eveleth, and Hibbing. Since the benefit and temperance associations often had overlapping memberships, they merged into a new national organization in 1920: the Order of Runeberg (*Runebergorden*). Lodges were subsequently organized in Biwabik, Chisholm, Eveleth, Hibbing, Minneapolis, West Duluth, and elsewhere. Temperance was dropped from the Runeberg bylaws in 1946, and fifteen years later the organization became the International Order of Runeberg. Runebergians now promote closer cultural ties with Finland's Swedish-speaking communities and encourage a greater awareness of the Finland Swedes' unique history within America.[150]

Today

Little evidence remains of the Finland Swedes' presence in Minnesota. The most recognizable place is Larsmont, where the residents' strong sense of community is displayed by the former schoolhouse, listed in the National Register of Historic Places in 1992. Elsewhere, the 1906 Baptist congregation established by Chisholm's Finland Swedes continues to serve the community, and the Lutheran congregations of French River and Palisade, founded jointly by Finland Swedes and Swedes, have not merged with nearby churches; those in Ely, Eveleth, Hibbing, and Virginia subsequently joined with other Lutherans to form new congregations.

In West Duluth, the exterior of the former Bethel Lutheran Church has changed relatively little over time, and the building still displays the stained-glass windows and names of those Finland Swedes who devoted time and resources to its development; the former sanctuary now houses offices. Nearby, another religious group occupies the former Ebenezer Baptist church building. The once-active Pentecostal

The former District No. 4 school in Larsmont, now a community center, was listed in the National Register of Historic Places in 1992.

tabernacle at Sheriff Lake remains a lonely sentinel on the landscape. All of the halls and societies once affiliated with the Finland Swedes' early temperance, benefit, and fraternal efforts in Minnesota are gone; and none of North America's twelve Runeberg lodges are located in the state. The primary organization serving the immigrants' descendants is the Swede-Finn Historical Society (SFHS), based in Seattle.

The Finland Swedes were a minority within a minority; as such, most North Americans had difficulty distinguishing them from Swedish or Finnish immigrants. As one chronicler noted in 1938, "To the American people the Finland Swedes are almost an unknown quantity." Some Finland Swedes also felt isolated in America: "the Swedes high-hat us and we can't talk to the Finns," bemoaned a Mesabi Range resident. Despite their small population, Minnesota's Finland Swedes maintained a distinctive ethnic identity within the state for almost a century. While it is inevitable that over time even fewer descendants of Finland Swedes will maintain connections to their heritage, the contributions of this small ethnic group to Minnesota's history merit further study and recognition.[151]

Personal Account:
Fred Torma (Törmä)

Fred Torma (1888–1979), a Finnish immigrant miner and carpenter, was a Socialist and cooperative leader in Nashwauk. Torma married Hilda Lampeä (1889–1959) in 1909, one year after she arrived from Alatornio, Finland. The couple had two children: Sylvia and William. Their son-in-law, Richard H. Silvola, whose parents were Finnish immigrants, served in Minnesota's House of Representatives from 1945 to 1953. The narrative is excerpted from a lengthy 1973 interview, conducted in Finnish by Douglas Ollila, Jr., and on deposit in the Finnish American Heritage Center and Historical Archive at Finlandia University (Hancock, MI). The much-abbreviated account has been edited and reorganized for clarity. Further biographical information was derived from the "Torma-Silvola Family Papers" at the Immigration History Research Center, University of Minnesota, and an account in the Finnish-language cooperative newspaper *Työväen Osuustomintalehti* [Superior, WI], 17 May 1956.

I heard about America when I was but a little boy, and at age 16 left for this country, arriving in Duluth on February 5, 1905. I immediately went to the Whiteside Lumber Company camp, where I worked three weeks for fifty cents a day. From there it was to the Stevenson Mine by Hibbing, where I was a carpenter's helper and received the lowest wage of $1.60 for a 12-hour day; out of that one had to pay for food and lodging. There was such a shortage of rooms that boardinghouse beds were used in two shifts. The vermin were a great problem, and it was impossible to get rid of lice. The odor from the barrel-shaped stove also came into the sleeping quarters, and laundry lines were everywhere. Later I worked in an open pit mine by Hibbing and shoveled ore into a high dump car. That was pretty heavy work for a sixteen-year-old, and dangerous, too. A rock could easily hit one on the head.

I always had the idea of a work people's hall in my heart because I had a socialistic upbringing in Finland. Since there were temperance halls in almost every town, we tried to take them over to further the cause of working people. The first time was at the Stevenson Mine, but the mining company intervened and drove us out. Then I went along the Mesabi Range, drifting from place to place before settling down in Aurora. When we Socialists tried to hold our meetings in the temperance hall the company asked the court to proclaim that no labor proceedings could occur there. After arriving in Nashwauk in 1906 I attended a Socialist meeting where I got the feeling that its members had a more far-reaching line of thought. Everyone agreed with my recommendation that we collect funds to build a small Socialist hall. Some thought we should merely put planks on top of beer kegs to serve as a stage, but I said we'll build a proper one for plays and speeches. I'd never been an actor but in that group one had to try. By 1910 the hall was too small, and some of the newer arrivals were aspiring actors who wanted to continue pursuing this avocation. I drew up the plans and once we got the hall enlarged 250 people could be crammed into it.

Hall activities occurred every evening. Committee meetings that planned out the week's programs took place on Mondays, while other committees ordered plays and produced them. We were so economical that only two scripts were ordered; the others were copied by hand. Play rehearsals were on Tuesday, dances on Wednesday, more play rehearsals on Thursday, debates on Friday, another dance on Saturday, and play performances on Sunday. Since no one could afford to purchase books, we established a library, which also was used by the debaters who needed information to defend their viewpoints.

My future wife's parents had been Laestadian Lutherans. When we started going together our ideological debates were quite fervent; but she was progressive minded, and quickly became an enthusiastic participant in hall activities, including teaching Finnish to the children. I've come to the conclusion that in Nashwauk hall activities had a much greater influence than churches did.

When the 1907 Mesabi strike began some of us went to the LaRue Mine; but the superintendent appeared with a long rifle and said: "If you step on company land I'll shoot." A few days later we were in the Finnish hall when the sheriff came to the door and shouted that if we wouldn't come out he'd shoot the hall into splinters. There were some old country knife fighters who said that they wouldn't leave and wanted to cut the sheriff's throat; however, I convinced them to leave peacefully. Since I was

Hilda Lempeä Torma and Fred Torma

put on the blacklist after the strike I didn't even try to work in Nashwauk. I went to a wet mine in Aurora, a terribly bad place. I worked a short time but quit since I felt that every joint in my body was stiff from the constant dampness.

I then went to work in the Dakotas, and on October 16 returned to Nashwauk, where I became a carpenter; in November I organized the Elanto cooperative boardinghouse that soon had 15 members. We rented a small private boardinghouse that included furniture and even a cow; but we fed the cow so much it became overweight and died. Since most boardinghouses never put eggs into the men's lunch pails, we started providing them for our members. Soon, men from elsewhere arrived in such numbers that we had to find a bigger building. This gave us more capital to establish a cooperative store. As treasurer I had to go to the store every evening and check the register, do the accounting work, take the money and put it under my pillow for the night, and bring it back in the morning. Our success was amazing as it was possible to obtain everything a person needed at the co-op.

I was a smith and a carpenter, having learned these skills during early boyhood. It's been a very good thing for me. If given a chance I could even make my life's breath from iron. Regardless of what has confronted me in America, I have been able to deal with it.

Further Reading

Durbin, William. *Song of Sampo Lake*. Minneapolis: University of Minnesota Press, 2011.

Eilola, Patricia. *A Finntown of the Soul*. St. Cloud: North Star Press, 2008.

Fisher, Thomas, and Peter Bastianelli-Kerze. *The Invisible Element of Place: The Architecture of David Salmela*. Minneapolis: University of Minnesota Press, 2011.

Hoglund, A. William. *Finnish Immigrants in America, 1880–1920*. Madison: University of Wisconsin Press, 1960.

Jalkanen, Ralph J., ed. *The Faith of the Finns: Historical Perspectives on the Finnish Lutheran Church in America*. East Lansing: Michigan State University Press, 1972.

Karni, Michael, and Aili Jarvenpa, eds. *Sampo: The Magic Mill: A Collection of Finnish-American Writing*. Moorhead, MN: New Rivers Press, 1989.

Karni, Michael G., Matte E. Kaups, and Douglas J. Ollila, Jr., eds. *The Finnish Experience in the Western Great Lakes Region: New Perspectives*. Minneapolis: Immigration History Research Center, University of Minnesota, 1975.

Karni, Michael G., and Douglas J. Ollila, Jr., eds. *For the Common Good: Finnish Immigrants and the Radical Response to Industrial America*. Superior, WI: Työmies Society, 1977.

Kero, Reino. *Migration from Finland to North America in the Years between the United States Civil and the First World War*. Turku, Finland: Institute for Migration, 1974.

Kivisto, Peter. *Immigrant Socialists in the United States: The Case of Finns and the Left*. Madison, NJ: Farleigh Dickinson University Press, 1984.

Laitala, Lynn Marie. *Up from Basswood*. Beaverton, ON: Aspasia Books, 1991.

Lemberg, Lauri. *St. Croix Avenue*. Trans. by Miriam Leino Eldridge. Superior, WI: Työmies Society, 1992.

Lockwood, Yvonne R. *Finnish American Rag Rugs: Art, Tradition & Ethnic Continuity*. East Lansing: Michigan State University Press, 2010.

Nordskaug, Michael, and Aaron W. Hautala. *The Opposite of Cold: The Northwoods Finnish Sauna Tradition*. Minneapolis: University of Minnesota Press, 2010.

Puotinen, Arthur. *Finnish Radicals and Religion in Midwestern Mining Towns, 1865–1914*. New York: Arno Press, 1979.

Ross, Carl. *The Finn Factor in American Labor, Culture and Society*. New York Mills, MN: Parta Printers, Inc., 1977.

Ross, Carl, and K. Marianne Wargelin Brown, eds. *Women Who Dared: The History of Finnish American Women*. Minneapolis: Immigration History Research Center, University of Minnesota, 1986.

Wasastjerna, Hans R., ed. *History of the Finns in Minnesota*. Trans. by Toivo Rosvall. Duluth: Minnesota Finnish-American Historical Society, 1957.

Notes

1. A. William Hoglund, *Finnish Immigrants in America, 1880–1920* (Madison: University of Wisconsin Press, 1960), 136. Here and elsewhere all census counts are based on published census documents from 1900 to 2000, the manuscript schedules for the 1860, 1870, 1880, 1900, 1910, 1920, and 1930 federal censuses, and the 1875, 1885, 1895, and 1905 Minnesota censuses. A figure for 2010 was derived from the American Community Survey, with assistance provided by Dan Veroff of the Applied Population Laboratory, UW-Madison/Extension.

2. Gary Kaunonen, *Finns in Michigan* (East Lansing: Michigan State University Press, 2009), 4.

3. Faith Fjeld, "About the North American Sámi," www.baiki.org/content/about. htm (accessed 10 Jan. 2009).

4. Terry G. Jordan and Matti E. Kaups, *The American Backwoods Frontier: An Ethnic and Ecological Interpretation* (Baltimore, MD: Johns Hopkins University Press, 1989), 56; Reino Kero, "Emigration from Finland to the United States," www.genealogia.fi/emi/emi3e.htm (accessed 17 Jan. 2006); communication from Auvo Kostiainen to author, 30 Jan. 2012.

5. Reino Kero, *Suureen Länteen: Siirtolaisuus Suomesta Pohjois-Amerikkaan* (Turku, Finland: Siirtolaisuusinstitituutti, 1996), 33–39, 147–48; manuscript census, 1860.

6. The Finns, called *Kvens* by the Norwegians, had been moving to Norway's Arctic fisheries for centuries. Solomon Ilmonen, *Amerikan Suomalaisten Historia ja Elämäkertoja*, Vol. 2 (Jyväskylä: K. J. Gummerus Osakeyhtiön kirjapainossa, 1923), 14–19, 40; Arnold R. Alanen, "The Norwegian Connection: The Background in Norway for Early Finnish Emigration to the American

Midwest," *Finnish Americana* 6 (1983–84): 23–33; John I. Kolehmainen, "Finnish Pioneers of Minnesota," *Minnesota History* 25 (Dec. 1944): 321; Vilho Reima, *Muistelmia siirtolaistemme vaelluksista ja elämästä* (Helsinki: K. F. Puromiehen Kirjapaino O. Y., 1937), 27.

7. Timo Riippa, "The Finns and Swede-Finns," in ed. June D. Holmquist, *They Chose Minnesota: A Survey of the State's Ethnic Groups* (St. Paul: Minnesota Historical Society Press, 1981), 297; Vilho Niitemaa, "The Finns in the Great Migratory Movement from Europe to America, 1865–1914," in eds. V. Niitemaa, et al., *Old Friends–Strong Ties* (Turku, Finland: Institute for Migration, 1976), 70; Kero, *Suureen Länteen*, 48–49.

8. Reino Kero, *Migration from Finland to North America in the Years Between the United States Civil War and the First World War* (Turku, Finland: Institute for Migration, 1974), 24–36; Kero, "Emigration from Finland"; Riippa, "Finns and Swede-Finns," 297–98.

9. Kero, "Emigration from Finland"; Kero, *Migration from Finland*, 92–93.

10. Kero, *Migration from Finland*, 23.

11. Matti Fred in *Sven Tuuva* [Hancock, MI], 27 Sept. 1878. *Pohjois-Suomi* [Oulu, Finland], 30 July 1879, cited in Kero, *Suureen Länteen*, 68.

12. *Oulun Wiikko-Sanomia* [Oulu, Finland], 30 May 1868, cited in Kero, *Suureen Länteen*, 41–42.

13. U.S. Department of Commerce, Bureau of the Census, *Fourteenth Census of the United States Taken in the Year 1920, V: Agriculture, Population, General Report and Analytical Tables* (Washington, DC: U.S. Government Printing Office, 1922), 319, 321.

14. Ralph Andrist, "Iron Man: The Finns

of Minnesota," unpublished manuscript, WPA collection, Minnesota Historical Society, St. Paul, 24–26; Ilmonen, *Historia,* 2:25, 132–42.

15. Ilmonen, *Historia,* 2:25–26; Andrist, "Iron Man," 24; Hans S. Wasastjerna, ed., *History of the Finns in Minnesota,* trans. Toivo Rosvall (Duluth: Minnesota Finnish-American Historical Society, 1957), 84–85.

16. Wasastjerna, *History of Finns,* 84, 91–92; Andrist, "Iron Man," 42; Solomon Ilmonen, *Amerikan Suomalaisten Historia,* Vol. 1 (Hancock, MI: Suomalais-Luteerilaisen kustannusliikkeen kirjapainossa, 1919), 163–64.

17. Wasastjerna, *History of Finns,* 93; Ilmonen, *Historia,* 1:164; Arnold R. Alanen, "In Search of the Pioneer Finnish Homesteader in America," *Finnish Americana* 4 (1981): 74; Andrist, "Iron Man," 27; Peter Lahti homestead application 3195, New Ulm–St. Peter Land offices, 1871 proof, National Archives and Records Administration, Washington, DC (hereinafter referred to as NARA).

18. Franklyn Curtiss-Wedge, *The History of Renville County, Minnesota* (Chicago: H. C. Cooper Jr. and Co., 1916), 990–91; Jon Gjerde, "The Development of Church Centered Communities among Three Minnesota Townships," MA thesis, University of Minnesota, 1978, 14–15; Riippa, "Finns and Swede-Finns," 298–99; manuscript censuses, 1870–1920; Warren Upham, "Renville–Finn Town Village," mnplaces.mnhs. org/upham/Results.cfm (accessed 20 Jan. 2012).

19. Lisa Thornquist, "Ethnic Settlement in Western Wright County, 1960–1905," MA thesis, University of Minnesota, 1984, 33; *Amerikan Suomalainen Lehti* [Calumet, MI], 12 Jan. 1883; Isaac Hare homestead application 1633 (abandoned), Greenleaf Land Office, NARA; *Cokato Enterprise,* 29 Jan. 1948; Reima, *Muistelmia,* citing Kärjenaho, 24.

20. Wasastjerna, *History of Finns,* 98–100;

Riippa, "Finns and Swede-Finns," 299; Ilmonen, *Historia,* citing Eva Barberg, 2:154; Isak Barberg homestead application 4516, Litchfield Land Office, 1875 proof, NARA.

21. Riippa, "Finns and Swede-Finns," 299.

22. Ilmonen, *Historia* 2, citing Barberg in *American Suomalainen Lehti,* 2, 9, 16 Jan. 1880; manuscript censuses, 1870, 1880.

23. Ilmonen, *Historia,* 2:186–91.

24. Piippo in *Uusi Kotimaa* [Minneapolis], 17 Dec. 1881.

25. Peter Julin homestead application 2933, Alexandria Land Office, 1873 proof, NARA; Wasastjerna, *History of Finns,* 115–16; *Amerikan Suomalainen Lehti,* 5 Dec. 1879 and 7 Nov. 1885; census reports and manuscript censuses, 1900–1920.

26. *Amerikan Suomalainen Lehti,* 8 Aug. 1879; interview with William Toivonen, 5 Oct. 2005.

27. Akseli Järnefelt, *Suomalaiset Amerikassa* (Helsinki: Osakeyhtiö Weilin & Göös Aktiebolag, 1899), 126; manuscript censuses, 1870, 1880; *Uusi Kotimaa* [New York Mills], 24 Dec. 1881.

28. *Amerikan Suomalainen Lehti,* 15 Sept. 1882; Järnefelt, *Suomalaiset Amerikassa,* 126; *Uusi Kotimaa,* 13 Oct. 1892.

29. Manuscript census, 1900.

30. *Amerikan Suomalainen Työmies* [Worcester, MA], 27 Jan. 1904; K. Marianne Wargelin, "Finntown, Minneapolis: An American Neighborhood," *Hennepin County History* (Fall 1988): 11; Minneapolis city directories, 1882–1900; manuscript census, 1900.

31. *Siirtolainen* [Duluth], 18 Dec. 1900; Työmies [Hancock, MI], 27 Aug. 1910 and 31 Aug. 1911; Wargelin, "Finntown," 9.

32. Julia Tumberg, *New York Mills Herald,* 27 Mar. 1930; *St. Paul Daily Pioneer,* 17 Dec. 1873; Matti Kaups, "Finns in Urban America: A View from Duluth," in ed. M. G. Karni, *Finnish Diaspora II: United States* (Toronto: Multicultural History Society of Ontario, 1981), 69.

33. Tumberg, *New York Mills Herald;*

Riippa, "Finns and Swede-Finns," 300–303; Ilmonen, *Historia*, 2:192–93, 201, 212.

34. Lähde in *Uusi Kotimaa*, 26 May 1887; *Siirtokansan Kalenteri* (Duluth: Yhdysvaltain ja Canadan Suomalainen Sanomalehtiliitto, 1922), 171.

35. Matti Kaups, "Finnish Place Names in Minnesota: A Study in Cultural Transfer," *Geographical Review* 56 (July 1966): 387, 391; Kip Peltoniemi, www.minnesotafinnish. org/index.asp?Type=B_BASIC&SEC (accessed 11 Aug. 2010).

36. Matti E. Kaups, "The Finns in the Copper and Iron Ore Mines of the Western Great Lakes Region, 1864–1905: Some Preliminary Observations," in eds. M. G. Karni, et al., *The Finnish Experience in the Western Great Lakes Region: New Perspectives* (Turku, Finland: Institute for Migration, 1975), 71.

37. Ilmonen, *Historia*, 2:222; Kaups, "Finns in Urban America," 69–70.

38. Kaups, "Finns in Urban America," 70, 77; census reports and manuscript censuses, 1880–1920.

39. Järnefelt, *Suomalaiset Amerikassa*, 131; *Duluth Evening Herald*, 7 Sept. 1900.

40. *Duluth Weekly Tribune*, 18 June 1880; *Amerikan Suometar*, 22 Sept. 1914; Wasastjerna, *History of Finns*, 209; Kaups, "Finns in Urban America," 69–70.

41. Manuscript census, 1910; Sanborn Fire Insurance Company map for Duluth, 1908, Duluth Public Library; Salo in *Työmies*, 27 Dec. 1911.

42. Salo in *Työmies*.

43. Manuscript census, 1910.

44. *Työmies*, 18 Aug. 1911, 12 Apr. 1912.

45. Kaups, "Finns in Urban America," 74; manuscript censuses, 1880–1930.

46. Kaups, "Finns in Urban America," 70–72; Duluth city directories, 1884–1914.

47. *Sosialisti* [Duluth], 2 Sept. and 18 Nov. 1914; *Siirtokansan Kalenteri* (Duluth: Minnesotan Suomalais-Amerikkalainen historiallinen seura, 1961), 155–56.

48. Hoover in *Duluth News-Tribune*, 31 Dec. 1939; 12 Dec. 1941; 28 Dec. 1941, Cosmopolitan section.

49. Paul Buffalo, "When Everybody Called me Gah-bay-bi-nayss: 'Forever-Flying-Bird.' An Ethnographic Biography of Paul Peter Bird," ed. Tim Roufs, www.d.umn. edu/cla/faculty/troufs/Buffalo/pbwww.html (accessed 8 Mar. 2010); Grace Lee Nute, *Rainy River Country: A Brief History of the Region Bordering Minnesota and Ontario* (St. Paul: Minnesota Historical Society Press, 1950), 92–93.

50. J. C. Ryan, *How Dark Is the Forest* (Duluth: St. Louis County Historical Society, 1983), 67; Hiram Drache, *Taming the Wilderness: The Northern Border Country, 1910–1939* (Danville, IL: Interstate Publishers, 1992), 32–43.

51. James M. Skibo and Michael Brian Schiffer, *People and Things: A Behavioral Approach to Material Culture* (New York: Springer, 2009), 33.

52. James P. Leary, ed., *So Ole Says to Lena: Folk Humor of the Upper Midwest*, 2nd ed. (Madison: University of Wisconsin Press, 2001), 125–26; a similar story is recounted in an interview with Jacob Pete, on file in Iron Range Research Center (hereinafter, IRRC), Chisholm.

53. James P. Leary and Richard March, "Farm, Forest, and Factory: Songs of Midwestern Labor," quotation by Pekka Granow and translation of Kyländer's song by Tellervo Zoller, in ed. Archie Green, *Songs about Work: Essays in Occupational Culture for Richard A. Reuss* (Bloomington: Folklore Institute, Indiana University), 268–71.

54. Walter O'Meara, *We Made It Through the Winter: A Memoir of Northern Minnesota Boyhood* (St. Paul: Minnesota Historical Society Press, 1974), 4–5, 15–16.

55. Nute, *Rainy River Country*, 92–93.

56. Arnold R. Alanen, "Years of Change on the Iron Range," in ed. C. E. Clark, Jr., *Minnesota in a Century of Change: The State and Its People Since 1900* (St. Paul: Minnesota Historical Society Press, 1989),

157–58; Pajari in *Deerwood Enterprise,* 9 May 1930; Gust Aakula in Wasastjerna, *History of Finns,* 139–40.

57. *Virginia Enterprise,* 3 July 1903; *Hibbing Tribune,* 13 Apr. 1900, 17 Mar. and 7 Apr. 1904; Polly C. Bullard, 1908 diary entry, Bullard Papers, Minnesota Historical Society, St. Paul; Ranta-Aho interview, undated WPA files, Minnesota Historical Society, St. Paul; Alanen, "Years of Change," 165.

58. Kaups, "Finns in the Mines," 71–73; manuscript censuses, 1885–1920.

59. Manuscript census, 1920.

60. Kaups, "Finns in the Mines," 80–86; Commissioner of Labor, *Eighth Biennial Report of the Bureau of Labor of the State of Minnesota, 1901–1902* (St. Paul: Pioneer Press Co., 1902), 361; Wasastjerna, *History of Finns,* 224–25; manuscript censuses, 1895–1910.

61. *Vermilion Iron Journal,* 18 Nov. 1884, 6 July 1893.

62. *Virginian* [Virginia, MN], 5 Aug. and 2 Sept. 1897, citing Pekkala; *Hibbing Sentinel,* 2 Oct. 1897.

63. *Tenth Biennial Report of the Bureau of Labor for the State of Minnesota, 1905–1906* (Minneapolis: Harrison and Smith Co., 1907), 449–53; *Eleventh Biennial Report of the Bureau of Labor, Industries and Commerce of the State of Minnesota, 1907–1908* (Minneapolis: Syndicate Printing Co., 1909), 172–73. The figure of three hundred was derived from reviews of all Iron Range newspapers, 1894–1905, and official reports thereafter.

64. Arnold R. Alanen, "Back to the Land: Immigrants and Image-Makers in the Lake Superior Region," in ed. G. F. Thompson, *Landscape in America* (Austin: University of Texas Press, 1995), 117.

65. Wasastjerna, *History of Finns,* 345–48; *Päivälehti* [Duluth], 24 Feb. 1948; manuscript census, 1880.

66. Matt Pelkonen, "The Palkie Mill," in *Siirtokansan Kalenteri* 52 (New York Mills: Minnesotan Suomalais-Amerikkalainen Historiallinen Seura, 1969), 49; John A. Mattinen, *History of the Thomson Farming Area,* trans. R. Impola (Cloquet: Carlton County Historical Soc., 2000), 119–21; Wasastjerna, *History of Finns,* 630–35; Ilmonen, *Historia,* 2:231; manuscript census, 1880.

67. Wasastjerna, *History of Finns,* 538–97; *Pelto ja Koti* [Superior, WI], June 1913, 27; manuscript census, 1900.

68. J. H. Jasberg, "Practical Colonization Work," *Proceedings of the Fourteenth Annual Meeting of the American Railway Development Association* (Denver, CO: The Association, 1922), 53–55; manuscript census, 1905; Wasastjerna, *History of Finns,* 628.

69. Wasastjerna, *History of Finns,* 538–97; Glanville Smith, "My Winter in the Woods," *Atlantic Monthly* (Apr. 1934): 419; manuscript censuses, 1900–20.

70. Wasastjerna, *History of Finns,* 199–204, 545–97; Lähde in *Uusi Kotimaa,* 4 June 1903; John Salmi, *Minnesota Lumberjack* (Detroit, MI: Harlo Press, 1971), 18.

71. Lily H. Beck, "Muistelmia lapsuusvuosiltani ja mietteitä musiikin merketyksestä," *Vappu* [Superior, WI], 1940, 26; Darrel H. Davis, "The Finland Community, Minnesota," *Geographical Review* 25 (July 1935): 382–94; Riippa, "Finns and Swede-Finns," 305.

72. Alanen, "In Search of the Homesteader," 83–84, and additional homestead records considered for this book.

73. Atami Kemppainen homestead 5047, Duluth Land Office, 1897 proof, NARA; manuscript census, 1900; Alanen, "In Search of the Homesteader," 80–81.

74. Allen G. Noble, *Wood, Brick, and Stone: Barns and Farm Structures,* Vol. 2 (Amherst: University of Massachusetts Press, 1984), 147; Arnold R. Alanen and William Tishler, "Finnish Farmstead Organization in Old World and New World Settings," *Journal of Cultural Geography* 1 (1980): 74–80.

75. Alanen and Tishler, "Finnish Farmstead Organization," 76–78.

76. Matti E. Kaups, "Finnish Log Houses in the Upper Middle West," *Journal of Cultural Geography* 3 (Spring/Summer 1983): 13.

77. Matti Kaups, "Finnish Meadow Hay Barns in the Lake Superior Region," *Journal of Cultural Geography* 10 (Winter 1989): 1–18.

78. Eugene Van Cleef, "The Finn in America," *Geographical Review* 6 (July 1918): 210; Matti Kaups, "A Finnish Savusauna in Minnesota," *Minnesota History* 45 (Spring 1976): 11–20; and the following, both by the Federal Writers' Project of the WPA, *Minnesota: A State Guide* (New York: The Viking Press, 1938), 292, and *The Minnesota Arrowhead Country* (Chicago: Albert Whitman and Co., 1941), 182.

79. Douglas Ollila, Jr., "Finnish-American Church Organizations," in Niitemaa, et al., *Old Friends–Strong Ties*, 152–53; Riippa, "Finns and Swede-Finns," 306; Jacob W. Heikkinen, *The Story of the Suomi Synod* (New York Mills: Parta Printers, Inc., 1985), 9.

80. *Amerikan Suomalainen Lehti*, 26 Sept. 1888; Riippa, "Finns and Swede-Finns," 306; Pekka Raittila, "Laestadianism in North America until 1885," and Jouko Talonen, "Laestadianism/Apostolic Lutheranism in North America Today," both in eds. A. Foltz and M. Yliniemi, *A Godly Heritage: Historical View of the Laestadian Revival and Development of the Apostolic Lutheran Church in America* (Frazee: privately published, 2005), 185–208.

81. Heikkinen, *Suomi Synod*, 56; Wasastjerna, *History of Finns*, 423–25; Riippa, "Finns and Swede-Finns," 306–7; Lillian H. Esala, *Directory of Churches of the Vermilion and Mesabi Iron Ranges of Northeastern Minnesota, 1884–1983* (Gilbert: Iron Range Historical Society, 1983), 40–41; message from Harry Lamppa to author, 13 Oct. 2011.

82. Riippa, "Finns and Swede-Finns," 306; Minnesota Historical Records Survey, WPA, *Directory of Churches and Religious Organizations in Minnesota*, ed. and ex-panded by Antona Hawkins Richardson (1942; St. Paul: Paduan Press, 1997), 105–6.

83. Riippa, "Finns and Swede-Finns," 307; Wasastjerna, *History of Finns*, 189, 220–21, 381–83, 452, 482, 486, 489, 495–97, 510–11, 561–62, 572, 580, 593–94, 596, 608, 640, 647; Mrs. Matt [Elin] Pitkanen, "The First Finnish Methodist Congregation in United States," in ed. C. N. Page, *Our Fathers Built: A Century of Minnesota Methodism* (Minneapolis: Historical Society of the Minnesota Methodist Conference, 1952), 131–34; Esala, *Directory*, 27.

84. Allan Pitkanen, trans. and ed., "Elin Durchman Pitkanen's Diary of her Migration Voyage to United States—October 9–28, 1911," *Finnish Americana* 3 (1980): 53; Pitkanen, "First Finnish Methodist Congregation," 132–33; Riippa, "Finns and Swede-Finns," 307; Richardson, *Directory of Churches*, 23–24, 121.

85. Carol Hepokoski, "Milma Lappala: Unitarian Minister and Humanist," in eds. Carl Ross and K. Marianne Wargelin Brown, *Women Who Dared: A History of Finnish American Women* (St. Paul: Immigration History Research Center, University of Minnesota, 1986): 158–64; Randall D. B. Tigue, "Labor and Lappala," in eds. D. M. Emerson and B. H. Smith, *Glorious Women: Award-Winning Sermons about Women* (Lincoln, NE: Ministerial Sisterhood Unitarian Universalist, 2004), quotation on 142–43.

86. Reino Kero, "Finnish Immigrant Culture in America," in Niitemaa, et al., *Old Friends–Strong Ties*, 115–16; Riippa, "Finns and Swede-Finns," 307.

87. Riippa, "Finns and Swede-Finns," 307–8.

88. Riippa, "Finns and Swede-Finns," 308.

89. Alfons Ukkonen, *A History of the Kaleva Knighthood and the Knights of Kaleva*, trans. T. Suurkuukka, ed. O. W. Saarinen (Beaverton, Ontario: Aspasia Books, 2002), 55–66, 71–72, 81–86, 99–107, 126–28, 145–46; *New World Finn* [Cedar Grove,

WI] 10 (Summer 2009): 6–7. Another camp, the Finlandia Beach Club, has also existed on Little Grand Lake since 1934; the camp was developed by a Cloquet Finnish workers' society, *Kehitys* ("Progress"), established in 1908.

90. Author's interviews with several Finnish Minnesotans, 1970s; Riippa, "Finns and Swede-Finns," 312.

91. *Duluth News-Tribune,* 17 Mar. 1940; Riippa, "Finns and Swede-Finns," 312.

92. Jaakko Paavolainen, "First-Generation Finnish-Americans Serve the United States," in Niitemaa, et al., *Old Friends–Strong Ties,* 248–55; Carl Ross, *The Finn Factor in American Labor, Culture and Society* (New York Mills: Parta Printers, Inc., 1977), 138–64; Kero, "Finnish Immigrant Culture," 118; Reino Kero, "Emigration from Finland," in eds. I. Semmingsen and P. Seerstad, *Scando-Americana Papers on Scandinavian Emigration to the United States* (Oslo: American Institute, University of Oslo, 1980), 63.

93. Peter Kivisto, *Immigrant Socialists in the United States: The Case of Finns and the Left* (London & Toronto: Associated University Presses, 1984), 16, 59–62, 92; Reino Kero, "The Roots of Finnish-American Left-Wing Radicalism," Institute of General History, University of Turku, Publication 5 (1973): 46.

94. Kivisto, *Immigrant Socialists,* 92, 95–98, 124; Auvo Kostiainen, "Finnish-American Workmen's Associations," in Niitemaa, et al., *Old Friends–Strong Ties,* 213–14.

95. Kivisto, *Immigrant Socialists,* 101–3; Kero, "Emigration from Finland," 58; Arnold R. Alanen, "Early Labor Strife on Minnesota's Mining Frontier, 1882–1906," *Minnesota History* 52 (Fall 1991): 246–63; manuscript censuses, 1905, 1910.

96. Michael G. Karni, "The Founding of the Finnish Socialist Federation and the Minnesota Strike of 1907," in eds. M. G. Karni and D. J. Ollila, Jr., *For the Common Good: Finnish Immigrants and the Radical Response to Industrial America* (Superior, WI: Työmies Society, 1977), 79–82; Peter Kivisto and Johanna Leinonen, "Representing Race: Ongoing Uncertainties about Finnish-American Racial Identity," *Journal of American Ethnic Studies* 31 (Fall 2011): 12; Wasastjerna, *History of Finns,* 477.

97. Kostiainen, "Finnish-American Workmen's Associations," 221–22; Douglas J. Ollila, Jr., "The Work People's College: Immigrant Education for Adjustment and Solidarity," in eds. Karni and Ollila, *For the Common Good,* 87–118.

98. Richard Hudelson and Carl Ross, *By the Ore Docks: A Working People's History of Duluth* (Minneapolis: University of Minnesota Press, 2006), 73–93; John E. Haynes, "Revolt of the 'Timberbeasts': IWW Labor Strike in Minnesota," *Minnesota History* 42 (Spring 1971): 162–74; Kivisto, *Immigrant Socialists,* 139–46; Ross, *Finn Factor,* 150–57.

99. Kostiainen, "Finnish-American Workmen's Associations," 221–29.

100. Kostiainen, "Finnish-American Workmen's Associations," 225–28; D. Jerome Tweton, *The New Deal at the Grass Roots: Programs for the People in Otter Tail County, Minnesota* (St. Paul: Minnesota Historical Society Press, 1988), 30–31; Hamilton Fish, *Investigation of Communist Propaganda,* House of Representatives, 71st Congress, Third Session, No. 2990 (17 Jan. 1931), 62; "Gus Hall," en.wikipedia.org/wiki/Gus_Hall (accessed 1 Apr. 2010).

101. Irina Takala, "From the Frying Pan Into the Fire: North American Finns in Soviet Karelia," *Journal of Finnish Studies* 8 (Aug. 2004): 109–11.

102. Mayme Sevander, with Laurie Hertzel, *They Took My Father: Finnish Americans in Stalin's Russia* (Minneapolis: University of Minnesota Press, 1992), 100.

103. Abraham Lincoln Brigade Archives, www.alba-valb.org (accessed 14 Feb. 2010); K. E. Heikkinen, ed., *Meidän poikamme espanjassa* (New York: Finnish Workers Federation, USA, Inc., 1939), translated in 2002

by Matti A. Mattson as *Our Boys in Spain*, 7; Jyrki Juusela, *Suomalaiset Espanjan sisallissodassa, 1936–39* (Jyväskylä, Finland: Atena Kustannus Oy, 2003), 219.

104. Maki biographical material from Carl Geiser Papers, Abraham Lincoln Brigade Archives, Tamiment Library, New York University.

105. Arnold R. Alanen, "A Remarkable Place, An Eventful Year: Politics and Recreation at Minnesota's Mesaba Co-op Park in 1936," *Journal of Finnish Studies* 8 (Aug. 2004): 67–86; Hudelson and Ross, *By the Ore Docks*, 189–93; Ross, *Finn Factor*, 173.

106. K. A. Nurmi, "The Cooperative Central Exchange and Its Possibilities for Expansion," in *Cooperative League of the USA, 1930 Yearbook* (New York: The League, 1930), 146.

107. Arnold R. Alanen, "The Development and Distribution of Finnish Consumers' Cooperatives in Michigan, Minnesota, and Wisconsin, 1903–1973," in Karni, et al., *The Finnish Experience*, 110–13.

108. Alanen, "Development of Finnish Cooperatives," 114; Erick Kendall, *And Into the Future: A Brief Story of Central Cooperative Wholesale's 25 Years of Building Towards a Better Tomorrow* (Superior, WI: Cooperative Publishing Association, 1945), 5.

109. Alanen, "Development of Finnish Cooperatives," 113–18; Eskel Ronn, "In Days of Old When Knights Were Bold," *Cooperative Pyramid Builder* [Superior, WI] 2 (Jan. 1927): 4.

110. Michael Karni, "Struggle on the Cooperative Front: The Separation of Central Cooperative Wholesale from Communism, 1929–30," in Karni, et al., *The Finnish Experience*, 186–201; Alanen, "Development of Finnish Cooperatives," 118–20; Cooperative League of the United States of America, *Third Yearbook* (Minneapolis: Northern States Cooperative League, 1936), 100–102; Central Cooperative Wholesale, *Yearbook 1943* (Superior, WI: Cooperative Publishing Association, 1943), 55; communication from Peter Kivisto to author, 4 May 2010.

111. Don Muhm, *More Than a Farm Organization: Farmers Union in Minnesota* (Rochester: Lone Oak Press, 1998), 66–75.

112. "The Country That Paid its Debts," *Embassy of Finland News*, 8 May 2006; *New York Times*, 15 July 1934.

113. Auvo Kostiainen, "Delaware as a Symbol of Finnish Immigration," *Turun Historiallinen Arkisto* 46 (1990): 49–70; *Official Program, Finnish Trecentenary Day, 300th Anniversary of First Finnish Settlement in America, Chester, PA* (1938), IHRC; *Cokato Enterprise*, 14 June 1938.

114. Wasastjerna, *History of Finns*, 278–83; Arne Halonen, "Minnesota's Help to Finland, $150,000 Contributed to Finnish Relief in Statewide Drive" (c. 1940), www.genealogia.fi/emi/art/article214e.htm (accessed 24 May 2010).

115. Halonen, "Minnesota's Help"; "Minneapolis Help Finland Program," 29 Dec. 1939, IHRC.

116. Wasastjerna, *History of Finns*, 282; Help Finland, Inc., materials in Finnish American Heritage Center and Historical Archive, Finlandia University, Hancock, MI.

117. Juha A. Kairikko and Jaakko Ruola, *White-tailed Deer in Finland* (Jyväskylä: Suomen Metsästäjäliitto, 2005), 42–47, 63–65.

118. Alanen, "Politics and Recreation," 83–84.

119. Ukkonen, *History of Kaleva Knighthood*; Alanen, "Development of Finnish Cooperatives," 121–30; Cloquet Cooperative Society Records, 1930–1978, Minnesota Historical Society, St. Paul.

120. Riippa, "Swedes and Swede-Finns," 307; "United in Christ for 100 Years, 1898–1998: History of United in Christ Lutheran Church, Eveleth, Minnesota" (Eveleth: The Church, 1998).

121. "The Present-Day Finnish American Community of Minneapolis–St. Paul," Minnesota Pages/Suomi-sivut, http://www.minnesotafinnish.org/index.asp?Type=B_BASIC&SEC={7F063445-D692-4905-9A5C-

9559149B8310} (accessed 8 Feb. 2012); the number of Laestadian/Apostolic Lutheran churches was derived from numerous websites.

122. Matti Kaups, "A Commentary Concerning the Legend of St. Urho in Minnesota," *Finnish Americana* 7 (1986): 13–17; Joanne Asala, compiler, *The Legend of St. Urho* (Iowa City, IA: Penfield Press, 2001).

123. "Welcome to FinnFest USA," www.finnfestusa.org/index.html (accessed 16 Sept. 2011).

124. "History of Salolampi Finnish Language Village & Salolampi Foundation," www.salolampi.org/foundation/foundationhistory.html (accessed 16 Sept. 2011); message from Marlene Salmela Banttari to author, 9 Dec. 2011.

125. See, for example, "The Best Countries in the World," *Newsweek*, 23 and 30 Aug. 2010, 30–34; Pasi Sahlberg, *Finnish Lessons: What We Can Learn from Educational Change in Finland* (New York: Teachers College Press, 2011); and Jenny Anderson, "From Finland an Intriguing School-Reform Model," *New York Times*, 12 Dec. 2011.

126. "Swedish-speaking Finns," en.wikipedia.org/wiki/Swedish-speaking_Finns, and "SFHS: The Swedish-Finn Historical Society," finlander.genealogia.fi/sfhswiki/index.php/Home_Page (both accessed 1 Sept. 2010).

127. Anders Myhrman, *Finlandssvenskar i Amerika* (Helsingfors: Svenska Litteratursällskapet i Finland, 1972), 247; and "The Finland-Swedes in America," *Swedish Pioneer Historical Quarterly* 31 (Jan. 1930): 17. The census sampling project, Integrated Public Use Microdata Series (IPUMS), is affiliated with the Minnesota Population Center (MPC), University of Minnesota.

128. Manuscript census, 1860; Myhrman, *Finlandssvenskar*, 254; Ilmonen, *Historia*, 2:180; *Siirtolainen* [Duluth], 18 Dec. 1900; *Työmies* [Hancock, MI], 27 Aug. 1910, 31 Aug. 1911; "Frederick, South Dakota,"

en.wikipedia.org/wiki/Frederick,_South_Dakota (accessed 12 Dec. 2010).

129. Manuscript census, 1920.

130. Manuscript census, 1920; Myhrman, *Finlandssvenskar*, 255–56.

131. Carl J. Silfversten, "History of the Bethel Lutheran Church," 1928, www.genealogia.org/emi/art/article390e.htm (accessed 4 May 2005).

132. Anders Myhrman, "The Finland-Swedes in Duluth, Minnesota," *Swedish Pioneer Historical Quarterly* 14 (Jan. 1963): 20–23; manuscript censuses, 1900–1920.

133. Manuscript census, 1920.

134. Manuscript census, 1920.

135. *Duluth News-Tribune*, 20 Oct. 1948; Carl F. Silfversten, "What is a Finland-Swede?" *Chisholm Tribune-Herald*, 23 June 1932; manuscript census, 1920.

136. Silfversten, "What is a Finland-Swede?"; manuscript census, 1920.

137. Timothy Cochrane and Hawk Tolson, *A Good Boat Speaks for Itself: Isle Royale Fishermen and Their Boats* (Minneapolis: University of Minnesota Press, 2002), 119; messages from Louis Mattson to author, 29 Aug. and 12 Oct. 2011; manuscript census, 1920; *Duluth News-Tribune*, 8 Aug. 1948; Silfversten, "What is a Finland-Swede?"; Tom Sjoblom, *The Autobiography of a Herring Choker* (privately published, 1991), 4–6.

138. Philip J. Anderson, "A Scandinavian Enclave on Lake Superior's North Shore: Settlement Patterns and Community Building among Norwegians, Swedes, and Swede Finns in Hovland, Minnesota," in eds. Philip J. Anderson and Dag Blanck, *Norwegians and Swedes in the United States: Friends and Neighbors* (St. Paul: Minnesota Historical Society Press, 2011), 247–50; manuscript census, 1920.

139. *Duluth Herald*, 6 June 1932; Eleanor Jackson Stone, *Hanging On: Homesteading in Cook County* (privately published, n.d.).

140. Myhrman, *Finlandssvenskar*, 255–56, 262–63; manuscript census, 1920.

141. Interview with John Terrance Kull-

hem, Russell Kullhem, and Henry Beck, 25 Oct. 2007; manuscript censuses, 1900–1920.

142. Myhrman, "Finland-Swedes in America," 31.

143. Silfversten, "History of Bethel."

144. Silfversten, "History of Bethel"; *Senior Reporter* [Duluth], Sept. and Nov. 1998.

145. *Duluth News-Tribune,* 24 Feb. 1908, 22 Mar. 1916; Myhrman, *Finlandssvenskar,* 248–49; Wasastjerna, *History of Finns,* 600.

146. Myhrman, *Finlandssvenskar,* 256–57, 262–63, Esala, *Directory,* 27; "The Beginning History of Chisholm Baptist," http://www.chisholm-baptist.org/16html (accessed 14 May 2011); Anderson, "National Register of Historic Places Nomination Form, Larsmont School," 1991, Historic Preservation Division, Minnesota Historical Society, St. Paul.

147. Esala, *Directory,* 34–41; Myhrman, *Finlandssvenskar,* 257–58, 262–63; *Ely Miner,* 5 Mar. 1975.

148. Richardson, *Directory,* 18; *Kirkollinen Kalenteri, 1916* (Hancock, MI: Suomalais-Luteerilainen Kustanusliike, 1915), 126; Kullhem-Beck interview; message from Rueben Anderson to author, 28 June 2008.

149. Myhrman, *Finlandssvenskar,* 267–68; Silfversten, "History of Bethel"; Kullhem-Beck interview.

150. Riippa, "Finns and Swede-Finns," 316; "History of the Order of Runeberg," www.orderofruneberg.org/aboutus/history.html (accessed 19 Sept. 2010).

151. Silfversten, "What is a Finland-Swede?"; John Sirjamaki, "Mesabi Communities: A Study of Their Development," PhD dissertation, Yale University, 1940, 259.

Notes to Sidebars

i. Wilhelm Carlson, *Pitäjänkertomuksia No. 4. Entinen Ikalinen: Historiallinen kertomus Ikalisten, Parkanon ja Kankaanpään pitäjistä* (Helsinki: Suomalaisen Kirjallisuuden Seuran kirjapainossa, 1871), 126–27, 139; Heikki Rantatupa, ed., *Parkanon ja Kihniön kirja* (Jyväskylä, Finland: K.J. Gum-

merus Osakeyhtiön kirjapainossa, 1971), 111; Samuli Onnela, "Suomalaiset Ruijan asuttajina," *Tornionlaakson vuosikirja* (1981): 270.

ii. Jenni Tuominen, "An Introduction to Finglish" (Tampere, Finland: Department of Translation Studies, University of Tempere, 2004), http://www.rocklin.ca/saarelaiset/finglish.htm; Pertti Virtaranta, *Amerikansuomen Sanakirja: A Dictionary of American Finnish* (Turku, Finland: Institute of Migration, 1992); *Virginia Enterprise,* 30 Aug. 1912; *Duluth News-Tribune,* 22 Feb. 1936; Bobby Aro, "King of the Great Northwoods," in *Kapakka in the Kaupunki* (Goofin' Records, 2006).

iii. Ilmonen, *Historia,* 2: 190; *Uusi Kotimaa,* 17 Dec. 1881.

iv. Alanen, "Years of Change," 176–77; V. S. Alanne, "Finnish Cooperative Boarding Houses and Hotels in the United States and Canada," *Fourth Yearbook of the Northern State's Cooperative League* (1928), 259–63; Kyyhkynen cited in *Duluth News-Tribune,* 27 Jan. 1954.

v. John I. Kolehmainen, "In Praise of the Finnish Backwoods Farmer," *Agricultural History* 24 (Jan. 1950): 3; Jasberg, "Practical Colonization Work"; Sebeka Centennial Committee, *Sebeka: One Hundred Years, 1888–1988* (Sebeka: The Committee, 1988): 342–45; Alanen, "Years of Change," 176–77; Hudelson and Ross, *By the Ore Docks,* 82–83; Alma Lunden, *Corduroy Roads* (privately published, 1979), 125; manuscript censuses, 1900, 1910, 1920.

vi. *Duluth News-Tribune,* 20 July 1941; Anderson information from Ina Pursi Alanen and Harold Jackman, 1980s; Mattinen, *Thomson Farming Area,* 173–76; Michael Karni, "Otto Walta: Finnish Folk Hero of the Iron Range," *Minnesota History* 40 (1967): 391–402; *Hibbing Tribune,* 23 and 25 Feb. 1905; Kaunonen, *Finns in Michigan,* 16.

vii. Francis M. Carroll and Franklin R. Raiter, *The Fires of Autumn: The Cloquet-Moose Lake Disaster of 1918* (St. Paul: Minnesota Historical Society Press, 1990);

Christine Skalko and Marlene Wisuri, *Fire Storm: The Great Fires of 1918* (Cloquet: Carlton County Historical Society, 2003); Glenn Maxham, *Hell Fire and Damnation ... in the Fires of 1918* (privately published, 2004).

viii. James A. Roe, "Virginia, Minnesota's Socialist Opera: Showplace of Iron Range Radicalism," *Finnish Americana* 9 (1992): 36–43; Wasastjerna, *History of Finns,* 245; Reino Hannula, *An Album of Finnish Halls* (San Luis Obispo, CA: Quality Hill Books, 1991); Sebeka Centennial Committee, *Sebeka,* 214–15; William Toivonen interview.

ix. *Duluth Tribune,* 5 and 14 May and 4 Sept. 1885; *Vermilion Iron Journal,* 5 Apr. 1894; *Duluth News-Tribune,* 9 Sept. and 1 and 7 Oct. 1918; *Truth* [Duluth], 4 and 11 Oct. 1918; Olli Kiukkonen's "Declaration of Intention" (1912) and "Certificate of Death" (1918), Minnesota Historical Society, St. Paul.

x. Jordan and Kaups, *Backwoods Frontier,* 89–92; Buffalo, "When Everybody Called me Gah-bay-bi-nayss"; Kivisto and Leinonen, "Representing Race," 14–15, 21–26.

xi. *Duluth News-Tribune,* 16 June 1913; *Duluth Herald,* 30 Dec. 1916; Hoglund, *Finnish Immigrants,* 98–99; *St. Paul Pioneer Press,* 16 Apr. 1925; Ralph H. Smith, *A Sociological Survey of the Finnish Settlement of New York Mills, Minnesota and Its Adjacent Territory,* MA thesis, University of Southern California, 1933, published: D. G. Nicholson, comp., (Minneapolis: Snellington Publishers, 2005), 125–32; *Voyageur Press* [McGregor], 2 Aug.

2005; Marvin G. Lamppa, *Those Fabulous Flying Finns* (Embarrass: Town of Embarrass/Sisu Heritage, 2005).

xii. Victor R. Green, *A Passion for Polka: Old-Time Ethnic Music in America* (Berkeley: University of California Press, 1992), 108–10; Ruth-Esther Hillila and Barbara Blanchard Hong, *Historical Dictionary of the Music and Musicians of Finland* (New York: Greenwood Press, 1997), 116; Joyce Hakala, *Memento of Finland: A Musical Legacy* (St. Paul: Pikebone Press, 1997); Michael Anthony, et al., *Osmo Vänskä: Orchestra Builder* (Minneapolis: Kirk House Publishers, 2009); Paul Metsa, *Blue Guitar Highway* (Minneapolis: University of Minnesota Press, 2011); *Duluth News-Tribune,* 3 July 1955.

xiii. Pamela A. Brunfelt, "Karl Emil Nygard: Minnesota's Communist Mayor," *Minnesota History* 58 (Fall 2002): 168–86; *Daily Worker* [New York City], 10 Dec. 1932; Elizabeth Oman, "Swede-Finns on the Iron Ranges of Northeastern Minnesota," *Finnish Americana* 7 (1986): 41; Myhrman, *Finlandssvenskar,* 269; "Governors of Minnesota," Finns text.docxwww.mnhs.org/people/governors/gov/gov_30.htm.

xiv. Tony Dierckins, et al., "Historic Duluth's East End Walking Tour" (Duluth: Duluth Preservation Alliance, 2010), http://www.duluthpreservation.org/EEWT-lowres.pdf; undated letter from A. W. Lignell to Maryanne Norton; messages from Maryanne Norton to the author, 29 and 31 Aug. 2011.

Index

Page numbers in *italic* refer to pictures and captions.

Illustration Source Details and Credits

page iv: Courtesy of Dan Reed / page vi: Raimo Hautanen, et al., *Skrabb-Tallbacka-suvun vaiheita*, Vol. 2 (privately printed), 2007; message from Toivo Kivipelto to author, 10 Aug. 2010. Photo by Arnold R. Alanen / page 3: Cartography by Department of Geography, University of Helsinki, Finland, and Kassie Martine / page 5, top: Thomas Fisher and Peter Bastianelli-Kerze, *Salmela Architect* (Minneapolis: University of Minnesota Press, 2005), 14–25. Photograph by Aaron W. Hatuala, from Michael Nordskog and Aaron W. Hautala, *The Opposite of Cold: The Northwood Finnish Sauna Tradition* (Minneapolis: University of Minnesota Press, 2010), 143 / page 5, bottom: Photo by Arnold R. Alanen / page 11: Matti Kaups Papers, Immigration History Research Center (University of Minnesota, Minneapolis) 1196, Box 26, Folder "Finn. Am. Originals" / page 13: Photo by Arnold R. Alanen / page 14: Cokato Historical Society / page 15: Courtesy Reino Kero / page 18 advertisements: Advertisements compiled from *Tyomies* [Superior, WI], Apr. 1937 / page 20–21, top: Minnesota Historical Society collections / page 20, bottom: Doug "Nils" Helppie, "The Helppie Family in Sebeka," in Sebeka Centennial Committee, *Sebeka*, 388–89. Photo from *Sebeka-Menahga Review Messenger* / page 21, bottom: Letter from Richard Alanen to author, 17 July 2010. Photo by Arnold R. Alanen / page 24: *Amerikan Albumi: Kuvia Amerikan suomalaisten asuinpaikiolta* (Brooklyn, NY: Suomalainen Kansalliskirjakauppa, 1904), 161 / page 25: A. William Hoglund Papers, Immigration History Research Center (University of Minnesota, Minneapolis) 3325, Box 86, Folder "Duluth" / page 27: Photograph by William J. Alanen; author's collection / page 29: Institute of Migration, Turku, Finland / page 33: Minnesota Historical Society collections / page 34: Jean Stolberg, ed., *Virginia, Souvenir Booklet: Virginia's Diamond Days Celebration, 1892–1967* (Virginia, MN: Diamond Jubilee Committee, 1967), 50; manuscript censuses, 1910, 1920. Photograph by Marilyn J. Chiat / page 37: Minnesota Historical Society collections / page 38: Matti Kaups Papers, Immigration History Research Center (University of Minnesota, Minneapolis) 1196, Box 28, Folder "Brimson" / page 39: Courtesy of the Carlton County Historical Society / page 40: Photograph by Ralph Wilen, courtesy of Dan Reed / page 41: Photo by Arnold R. Alanen / page 42, top: Minnesota Historical Society collections / page 42, bottom: Matti Kaups Papers, Immigration History Research Center (University of Minnesota, Minneapolis) 1196, Box 28, Folder "Hay meadow barns" / page 43: Photo by Arnold R. Alanen / page 44: Matti Kaups photographer; Matti Kaups Papers, Immigration History Research Center (University of Minnesota, Minneapolis) 1196, Box 21, Folder "Savusaunas" / page 45: Minnesota Historical Society collections / page 46: Communication from Elmer and Miriam Yliniemi, 30 Dec. 2011. Photo by Arnold R. Alanen / page 48: Finnish American Heritage Center and Historical Archive at Finlandia University, Hancock, MI / page 52: *Duluth Herald*, 10 June 1922 / page 53, top: Photo by Arnold R. Alanen / page 53, bottom: Courtesy of Paul Niemisto / page 56: *Tie Vapauteen* [Duluth], 13 (Apr. 1931), 48 / page 57: Photo by Arnold R. Alanen / page 59: *Deadwood* [South Dakota] *Pioneer*, 14 Oct. 1934; *Fergus Falls Daily Journal*, 16 Oct. 1934; State of Minnesota, Adjutant General's Office, Graves Registration Section, Minnesota Historical Society, St. Paul; manuscript censuses, 1910, 1920, 1930. Photo by Arnold R. Alanen / page 61: Hudelson and Ross, *By the Ore Docks*, 210–14, 246; Millard R. Gieske, *Minnesota Farmer-Laborism: The Third Party Alternative* (Minneapolis: University of Minnesota Press, 1979), 326–27. Photo from Minnesota Historical Society collections / page 62: Alanen, "A Remarkable Place, An Eventful Year," 74–79. Photo courtesy of the Mesaba Co-operative Park Association / page 63: Author's collection / page 67: Help Finland, Inc., materials in Finnish American Heritage Center and Historical Archive at Finlandia University, Hancock, MI / page 68: Courtesy of Carl Gawboy / page 69: Bois Forte Band of Chippewa Communication Office / page 70: "Taisto Elo," in Kenneth J. Enkel Papers, Immigration History Research Center, University of Minnesota, Minneapolis. Photo courtesy of Suzanna Raker / page 71: *Pine Journal* [Cloquet], 26 May 2011; *Duluth News-Tribune*, 29 May 2011; "Dale Eugene Wayrynen," *Wikipedia* (accessed 6 June 2010). Photo in author's collection / page 72: Pete Sieger / page 73: Courtesy of the Carlton County Historical Society / page 74: Photo by Arnold R. Alanen / page 75: Wasastjerna, *History of Finns*, 654–56; "Toasts of the President and President Kekkonen. October 16, 1961," www.jfklink.com/speeches/jfk/publicpapers/1961/jfk422_61.html. Photo courtesy Esko Historical Society / page 76: Beatrice A. Ojakangas, *The Finnish Cookbook*

(New York: Crown Publishers, Inc., 1984). Photo from Star Tribune/Minneapolis–St. Paul, 2012 (published 27 Jan. 2010) / page 81, top: Photo by Sigfred Nygard; courtesy of the Nygard family / page 81, bottom: Minnesota Historical Society collections / page 82: *Duluth News-Tribune*, Cosmopolitan Section, 24 Aug. 1941; manuscript censuses, 1900–1930. Photo courtesy Arthur Englund / page 83: Photo by Arnold R. Alanen / page 84: Cochrane and Tolson, *A Good Boat Speaks for Itself*, 81, 83, 97, 111, 116, 122, 140–44, 149–50, 174–76. Photo courtesy of Randy Ellestad / page 86: Olga Bergström Passenger Record, Institute of Migration, Turku, Finland; biographical information about Olga and Edwin Petrell provided by JoAnn Hanson. Photo courtesy of JoAnn M. Hanson, PhD / page 87: Photo courtesy of Larry Fortner / page 89: *Svensk-Finska Nykterhet-Forbundet af Amerika i Ord och Bild* (Chicago?: Svensk-Finska Nykterhets-Förbundet, 1908), 90 / page 90: *Minnesskrift Svensk-Finska Nykterhetsförbundet av Amerika, 1902–1917* (Chicago: J. V. Martensons tryckeri, 1917), 81 / page 92: Photo by Arnold R. Alanen / page 95: *Työväen Osuustomintalehti* [Superior, WI], 17 May 1956

Acknowledgments

I am indebted to Lynn Bjorkman for editorial advice, moral support, and thoughtful observations while traveling throughout northeastern Minnesota and Finland; to Hannele Jönsson-Korhola and Sinikka Santala for checking my Finnish translations; to Richard Alanen for accompanying me on trips within the "Finnish Triangle"; to Auvo Kostiainen for always responding to my detailed questions about Finns on both sides of the Atlantic; to Syrene Forsman for providing information about Finland Swedes; to Lynette Neitzel, Aaron Hautala, Jouni Korkeasaari, Rachel Martin, and Daniel Necas for photo preparation; and to Maija and Marit Alanen for understanding, on our travels, why we always stopped to look at another Finnish building or talk to one more person who might have an interesting personal story.

Debbie Miller of the Minnesota Historical Society helped resolve some of my most perplexing research problems, while Shannon Pennefeather, managing editor of the Minnesota Historical Society Press, deserves special recognition for her patience, good judgment, and excellent editing skills throughout the publication process.

The following individuals offered valuable information about specific Finnish localities and people in Minnesota, reviewed sections of the manuscript, and/or provided images. I extend my thanks to all of them. Any omissions are entirely unintentional.

Arvo William Alanen, Rueben Anderson, Soile Anderson, Mike Aro, Paul Bankord, Marlene Salmela Banttari, Harvey Barberg, Henry Berg, Katherine Bergan, Pamela Brunfelt, Marilyn Chiat, Timothy Cochrane, Jeanne Santa Doty, Joan Mickelson Dwyer, Randy Ellestad, Arthur Englund, Faith Fjeld, Larry Fortner, Carl Gawboy, JoAnn D. Hanson, E. Haven Hawley, Gary Hill, Janet Sha Hill, Richard Hudelson, Abner Jonas, Kathleen Ristinen Jonas, Gary Kaunonen, Reino Kero, Melvin Kinnunen, Toivo Kivipelto, Peter Kivisto, Olavi Koivukangas, Rebecca Komppa, Michael Koop, Martin Kotila, John Terrance Kullhem, Russell Kullhem, James Kurtti, Harry Lamppa, James W. Larson, James Leary, Mary Lukkarilla, Maija Mäki-Laurila, Clifford Matta, Louis Mattson, Patricia Maus, Carolyn Johnson Mayo, Bryan McGinnis, Karin Hertel McGinnis, Halyna Myroniuk, Ivy Koskell Nevala, Darrell Nicholson, Juha Niemelä, Paul Niemisto, Michael Nordskog, Maryanne Norton, Beatrice Luoma Ojakangas, Kip Peltoniemi, Gabriel Pipo, Roy Pipo, Suzanna Raker, Kent Randell, Kate Roberts, Heikki Rouvinen, David Salmela, Peter Sieger, Raimund Silja, Ismo Söderling, Jacqueline Vesel Solem, Larry Sommer, Richard Sundberg, Ellen Sundholm, Audrey Ryti Tack, Carolyn Torma, Beth Virtanen, Hilary Virtanen, Marianne Wargelin, Betty Lake Warren, Margaret Olson Webster, Helen Wilkie, Warner Wirta, Marlene Wisuri, Lydia Woods, Joel Wurl, Elmer Yliniemi, and Miriam Suomala Yliniemi.

I also have had the great privilege to know several individuals who are no longer with us but whose ideas, insights, and publications still influence my scholarly endeavors: A. William Hoglund, Machael Karni, Matti Kaups, John Kolehmainen, Douglas Ollila, Jr., Timo Riippa, Carl Ross, and Rudolph Vecoli.

Partial research funding for this book was provided by Finlandia Foundation National (US) and the Institute of Migration (Finland).

Minnesotans can trace their families and their state's heritage to a multitude of ethnic groups. *The People of Minnesota* series tells each group's story in a compact, handsomely illustrated, and accessible paperback. Readers will learn about the group's accomplishments, ethnic organizations, settlement patterns, and occupations. Each book includes a personal story of one person or family, told through a diary, a letter, or an oral history.

Minnesota writer Bill Holm reminded us why these stories remain as important as ever: "To be ethnic, somehow, is to be human. Neither can we escape it, nor should we want to. You cannot interest yourself in the lives of your neighbors if you don't take sufficient interest in your own."

This series is based on the critically acclaimed book *They Chose Minnesota: A Survey of the State's Ethnic Groups* (Minnesota Historical Society Press). The volumes in *The People of Minnesota* bring each group's story up to date and add dozens of photographs to inform and enhance the telling.

Books in the series include *Swedes in Minnesota, Jews in Minnesota, Norwegians in Minnesota, African Americans in Minnesota,* and *Germans in Minnesota.*

About the Author

Arnold R. Alanen, who holds a PhD in cultural geography from the University of Minnesota, is a professor emeritus of landscape architecture at the University of Wisconsin–Madison and a third-generation Finnish American from Minnesota. He has written extensively on the topics of landscape history, vernacular architecture, settlement patterns of Finnish Americans, and cultural resource preservation.